RULERS OF INDIA

Owing to the antiquity and rarity of this book, certain pages are regrettably absent, and readability is compromised due to the blurring of the original text. If you possess any insights regarding the availability of these missing sections, kindly inform us. Your assistance is crucial in ensuring the completion of this significant work for the benefit of future generations.

RULERS OF INDIA

THE MARQUESS CORNWALLIS

W. S. SETON-KARR

GYAN

Published by

GYAN

Gyan Publishing House
5, Ansari Road
Daryaganj, New Delhi-110002
Phone: 011-47034999, 9811692060
E-mail: books@gyanbooks.com

Distribution Network
gyanbooks.com
India, USA, Canada, UK, Australia

ISBN: 978-93-7414-385-8 (PB)

First Published, 1890

2nd Impression 2025

Printed at: Gyan Press, Delhi.

RULERS OF INDIA
Author: W. S. SETON-KARR

RULERS OF INDIA

The Marquess Cornwallis

By W. S. SETON-KARR, Esq.

FORMERLY A PUISNE JUDGE OF THE HIGH COURT OF CALCUTTA
AND SOMETIME SECRETARY TO THE GOVERNMENT OF INDIA
IN THE FOREIGN DEPARTMENT

Oxford

AT THE CLARENDON PRESS: 1890

Oxford
PRINTED AT THE CLARENDON PRESS
BY HORACE HART, M.A.
PRINTER TO THE UNIVERSITY

Rulers of India

EDITED BY

SIR WILLIAM WILSON HUNTER, K.C.S.I., C.I.E.

M.A. (Oxford): LL.D. (Cambridge)

LORD CORNWALLIS

CONTENTS

NOTE

The orthography of proper names follows the system adopted by the Indian Government for the *Imperial Gazetteer of India.* That system, while adhering to the popular spelling of very well-known places, such as Punjab, Lucknow, etc., employs in all other cases the vowels with the following uniform sounds:—

a, as in wom*a*n: *á*, as in f*a*thers: *i*, as in pol*i*ce: *í*, as in intr*i*gue: *o*, as in c*o*ld: *u*, as in b*u*ll: *ú*, as in s*u*re: *e*, as in gr*e*y.

LORD CORNWALLIS

CHAPTER I

Early Life and American Campaign

The family of Cornwallis, Mr. Ross says with truth, was of some importance in Ireland, as is shown by the family papers. The first of whom we hear anything positive in England was Thomas Cornwallis, who became Sheriff of London in 1378. He acquired property in Suffolk, and his son and grandson represented that county in Parliament. One of his successors helped to suppress the insurrection of Wyatt, and was rewarded by the office of Treasurer of the Household. The grandson of the Treasurer was created a baronet by Charles I, supported the Royal cause, and followed Charles II to the Continent. After the Restoration, Sir Frederick became Baron Cornwallis in 1661. The third holder of this title is known as having married Anne Scott, widow of Monmouth and Duchess of Buccleugh. The fifth baron, who was Chief Justice of Eyre south of Trent, and Constable of the Tower, was created Earl Cornwallis and Viscount Brome in June, 1753. His son, born December 31, 1738, is the subject of the present memoir.

Charles, second Earl and first Marquess Cornwallis, was educated at Eton; and, according to the custom of the time, entered the army at the age of eighteen. He was sent abroad in 1757 to acquire some technical knowledge, and joined the Military Academy at Turin. Several amusing anecdotes of his life there are given in letters from a Prussian officer, Captain De Roguin, who appears to have accompanied the young Englishman as a sort of travelling companion and tutor. The discipline of the Academy seems to have been fairly strict, and Lord Brome spent his time in learning to dance and fence, studying the German language, and taking lessons in the riding school. After leaving Turin he visited some of the German courts, served on the staff of Lord Granby, and was present at several actions on the Continent, including the battle of Minden. In 1760 he entered Parliament as member for Eye, but in less than two years he succeeded to the earldom, on the death of his father in June, 1762.

Hitherto there had been nothing extraordinary in the career of Earl Cornwallis. He had benefitted by a public school education. His mind had been opened and his taste improved by foreign travel, and he had seen some hard service at Minden, Labinau, and other minor actions against the French. On his return home he continued to pay attention to his military duties and was stationed with his regiment at Dublin, Derby, Gloucester, and Gibraltar. In July, 1768, he married Jemima, daughter of Colonel Jones of the third regiment of Foot Guards. He seems to have been constantly in his place in the House of Peers, and to have voted usually with Lord Shelburne, who eventually became the first Lord Lansdowne, and with Earl Temple. It is significant that notwithstanding the political opinions of his predecessors he was steadily opposed to the scheme for taxing the American colonists, and though he held divers Ministerial appointments he voted against the Ministry of the day on more than one occasion. In 1770 he was violently denounced by Junius, and by that venomous writer was credited with the intention of 'retiring into voluntary banishment in the hope of recovering some of his reputation.'

This attack rests on no more basis of truth than many of the accusations of Junius. But so far from retiring from public life into social exile, it was the fate of Cornwallis from this date to take a decided and prominent part in most important events in America, in India, in Ireland, and on the Continent. Practically, his public career may be divided into four portions. He commanded a division of Royal troops and saw much service in the American War of Independence. He was Governor-General and

Commander-in-Chief in India—first from September, 1786, to October, 1793, and again from July to October, 1805. He was Lord-Lieutenant and Commander-in-Chief in Ireland for nearly three years—between June, 1798 and May, 1801. He negotiated the Peace of Amiens.

It will be the object of this memoir to describe the aims, motives, and character of Lord Cornwallis as an Indian Ruler, and to notice the historical events with which he was connected only so far as may be necessary for the comprehension of his character. Average English readers must be credited with a fair knowledge of the struggle which led to the loss of our American colonies, with the condition of Ireland at the beginning of the present century, and with the French war terminated by the short Peace of Amiens. Similarly, in treating of the Indian administration there will be no detailed account of the two successive campaigns waged against Tipú Sultán. But to the important measures of reform in India introduced by Lord Cornwallis a considerable space will be accorded. And, generally speaking, no facts or anecdotes will be omitted which tend to assign to this statesman his due place in history, whether as a soldier or a civil administrator.

Cornwallis, who by this time had attained the rank of Lieutenant-General, was directed to take command of a division of the English army in America at the beginning of 1776. He had opposed the Ministry and regretted the contest, but under a sense of military duty he accepted the post. Two years afterwards we find him in England. He returned to America in April, 1778, but again came home and threw up his command; not from any conviction of the injustice of the war, but owing to the illness of Lady Cornwallis, who pined in the absence of her husband and died at Culford, the family place, on February 14, 1779.

This sad event decided him to return to active service, and he was again employed in America till his surrender at York Town. The late Sir John Kaye holds the opinion that our success in America had become hopeless even before the first arrival of Cornwallis. And the prospect became still darker when the chief command was entrusted to Sir Henry Clinton in succession to Sir William Howe. According to the late Lord Stanhope, we should not have laid the foundations of our Empire in Bengal but for Clive, and the historian adds that had Clive lived we might not have lost our American colonies; or at least their independence would have been attained in some other way. While it is almost needless to state that in America we had no heaven-born general on our side, it is fair to add that Cornwallis met and fairly defeated the colonists on at least three occasions.

When the English forces had evacuated Philadelphia with some loss of stores and more loss of honour, Cornwallis, in his first campaign, repulsed the Americans who were closing round his rear with no inconsiderable loss. At the siege of Charleston he actually as a volunteer formed one of the storming party, and if it be objected that a general officer had no business to place himself in such a position, his example was followed by Sir James Outram in the Indian Mutiny, who charged with the Volunteer Cavalry at the relief of Lucknow and actually resigned the command to General Havelock. On August 18, 1780, by a rapid march from Charleston to Camden and Rugeley Mills, he totally defeated the army of General Gates. In a letter to an officer he says: 'Above 1000 were killed and wounded and about 800 taken prisoners. We are in possession of eight pieces of brass cannon, all they had in the field, all their ammunition-waggons, a great number of arms, and 130 baggage-waggons: in short, there never was a more complete victory.' Unfortunately, as has been remarked by more than one writer, these temporary successes were never properly followed up. Our movements were hindered by want of transport and by a defective commissariat; and the British army, though numerically superior to its adversaries, was never strong in discipline or *morale*. Moreover, while Cornwallis was successful, detachments under other officers were defeated by the colonists. The Royalists and their levies of militia became dispirited and disheartened by a series of small failures, and although the campaign of 1780 was on the whole favourable to the Royal cause, Colonel Tarleton suffered a defeat at

Cowpens, which has been described as the most serious calamity after the surrender of Saratoga. What could be done to repair this defeat was done by Cornwallis. At Guildford he attacked General Greene, who commanded a force of nearly 6000 men, and on March 15, 1781, he routed this officer and captured his cannon. But here again want of supplies, the general disaffection of the country, and the failure of energy on the part of the Loyalists, crippled operations; and although this action is admitted by the American writers to have been a 'signal instance of the steadiness of British troops when well commanded,' and though one English annalist compares it to Cressy, Poitiers, and Agincourt, it was only an apparent triumph; and indeed it may be said to have inflicted more damage on the English than on the Americans.

Cornwallis, who had been wounded in the battle of Guildford, next marched through North Carolina into Virginia, and took up his position at York and Gloucester, on the York River. It is not easy to apportion the blame for the surrender of York Town. The Commander-in-Chief subsequently endeavoured to show that he had not thought favourably of Cornwallis's march into the Virginian provinces. But it is quite clear that he ordered Cornwallis to act on the defensive and to fortify himself in some suitable position. Cornwallis had also some hope of relief or assistance from the British fleet. But nothing was done with vigour and effect. And when the American and French armies, strong in men and material, artillery and engineers, closed round the English forces, nothing was left for the Commander but to surrender his post or to try and cut his way out through the enemy. When the latter alternative had been tried in vain, the surrender of an exhausted garrison and crumbling works naturally followed.

This event practically put an end to the contest. Cornwallis remained a prisoner of war for about three months and was allowed to leave on parole for England. It is pleasant to note that in his letters he mentions with gratitude and good-feeling the delicacy and courtesy shown to him and others by the French officers. Eventually, after a long and troublesome correspondence about his exchange with Colonel Laurens, an American prisoner of high rank, he was released from his parole at the beginning of 1783.

Without analysing the numerous pamphlets and letters in which the responsibility for our failure was long and acrimoniously discussed, it is quite possible to form an estimate of the merits of Cornwallis as a military man and a strategist. That he did not possess the quick perception and the rapid glances which distinguish great captains in the field, may be readily admitted. But there is every reason to think that under a first-rate commander, Cornwallis at the head of a division, or despatched to carry out some distinct combination, or to operate in a particular quarter with adequate support, might have won no inconsiderable military distinction.

He had been well trained; he was a good disciplinarian; he knew when and how to be severe, and he had formed some distinct idea of carrying on a campaign. Sir H. Clinton showed his incapacity by recommending desultory measures as a means of reducing the enemy. Cornwallis tells us that he was quite tired of 'marching about the country in quest of adventures.' He informs his Commander-in-Chief that the right maxim for the safe and honourable conduct of the war was 'to have as few posts as possible, and that wherever the King's troops are, they should be in respectable force.' He was in favour of offensive operations in Virginia only. He did not foresee the least advantage from destroying goods and property at Philadelphia. He thought it absurd to attempt to turn an unhealthy swamp into a defensive post, which could at once be taken by an enemy with a temporary superiority at sea. In fact, he was for concentrating his efforts on operations in a province where a decisive victory would mean the defeat of his opponents; and at one time before the surrender of York Town we had firm possession of four important provinces, while another state, Vermont, had shown a desire for union with Canada. Our Loyalists had not then lost all heart, and the 'Americans were reduced to great straits for both money and supplies.'

In a very few years, however, the talents and

experience of Cornwallis were to find scope for their action in a very different sphere, where he would not be hampered by the incapacity of a superior, and where what Gibbon terms the seals and the standard, or the civil and military power, would be vested in the same person. We have it on his own authority that Lord Shelburne in May, 1782, proposed to him 'to go to India as Governor-General and Commander-in-Chief.' It is clear from this, that notwithstanding the disaster of York Town, Cornwallis still possessed the confidence of statesmen high in office, and was thought fitted for important trusts. Yet about the same time we find him complaining that he had been treated very unfairly by the King and Mr. Pitt, and that these two great personages had agreed to expose him to the world 'as an object of contempt and ridicule.'

It seems from the correspondence that negotiations with a view to engage Cornwallis in the Administration were not very delicately and judiciously managed. It is curious too that Cornwallis, when turning over the suggestion of India in his mind, should have come to the conclusion that it offered no field for military reputation. Possibly the recollection of failures in America may have warped his judgment, and the recent defeat and capture of our officers by Haidar Alí may have obliterated the memories of Plassey and Baxár.

Cornwallis writes thus to Colonel Ross in anticipations which happily were not fulfilled. He does not feel inclined 'to abandon my children and every comfort on this side the grave, to quarrel with the Supreme Government in India, whatever it may be: to find that I have neither power to model the army nor to correct abuses; and finally, to run the risk of being beaten by some Nabob and disgraced to all eternity.' Cornwallis may have been thinking of the wearisome disputes between Hastings and Francis, and the support withheld by other members of the Council from the Governor-General.

In June, 1784, there came a distinct intimation that the Ministers intended to offer him the two posts of Governor-General and Commander-in-Chief, and in February, 1785, he was 'attacked,' as he phrases it, to take the Governor-Generalship. To this proposal, after a consideration of twenty-four hours, he gave a 'civil negative.' This it might be thought would have precluded any renewal of similar negotiations, and during the next year Cornwallis was much taken up with the claims to compensation preferred by the American loyalists, and by the proceedings of a Board or Special Commission for the fortification of our sea-ports, of which, with other distinguished naval and military officers, he was made a member. In the same year he was deputed to Berlin to attend a review of the Prussian army, and was received there with some civility by Frederic the Great, though it is expressly mentioned in a letter to Colonel Ross that the king showed a marked preference for La Fayette. A conversation between the king and the English General, recorded in the Cornwallis *Correspondence*, is very curious as showing Frederic's view of the political relations of continental states with each other and with England.

In the beginning of 1786, from some cause not clearly explained in Cornwallis's *Life and Letters*, the offer of India was again made, and with grief of heart, as he puts it, Cornwallis accepted the appointment, sailed in May, and landed in Calcutta in September of the same year. A Bill, on lines which he had himself approved or suggested, enlarging the powers of the Governor-General under the India Bill of 1783, and very properly giving him authority to act on emergencies without the concurrence of his Council, and even in opposition to that body, received the Royal assent after his departure for the East.

CHAPTER II

POLITICAL CONDITION OF INDIA. THE REVENUE SETTLEMENT

A SHORT summary of the condition of British India at that time may not be deemed superfluous for the complete understanding of the powers, responsibilities, and policy of the new Governor-General.

We had acquired and had begun in a fashion to administer the fine provinces of Bengal and Behar with a portion of Orissa. The six great Maráthá houses with large territories and disciplined forces were still independent. Muhammadan Viceroys ruled over vast tracts of country at Lucknow and at Haidarábád. There were other lesser Nawábs of the Karnatic and of Farukhábád, and Rájás at Travancore and Tanjore, who at any moment might require support and countenance as allies,—if they did not become troublesome as enemies. The Presidency of Bombay was comprised within two islands, and some not very important districts on the mainland. Madras was more extensive; but over the greater portion of India, dynasties, old and young, and potentates of every degree of merit, demerit, and obscurity, still held sway, and their representatives were ever ready to appropriate to themselves some share in a Mughal empire which when at its highest had lasted only a century and a half, and was now crumbling to pieces.

Before dealing with any of the reforms in civil administration carried out by Cornwallis, it is as well to state briefly the result of two campaigns waged against our bitterest and most formidable opponent. Tipú Sultán, the son of Haidar Alí who had supplanted the old Hindu Rájás of Mysore and ruled at Seringapatam. The war began under the auspices of General Medows as Commander-in-Chief at Madras. Tipú had made an unprovoked attack on our ally the Rájá of Travancore, and it was the object of the General, in alliance with the Nizám and the Peshwá, to bring the Sultán to account. But it soon appeared that Medows, though a brave, experienced, and chivalrous officer, had not the strategic qualities which, in a difficult country and against a watchful and wary enemy, were sufficient to ensure success. To add to this, our army was badly equipped and provisioned. The Treasury was empty. The civil government of Madras was incapable. At the close of the year 1790, Cornwallis, the Governor-General, made use of his provisional powers and practically assumed command of the army in the field.

It is creditable to Medows that he displayed no resentment at his supersession, and that he continued to carry out the orders of Cornwallis with perfect cordiality and fidelity. In March, 1791, Bangalore was stormed, and Tipú fell back on Seringapatam. Cornwallis followed. But when within ten miles of that city, although he had met and dispersed the enemy in the field, he found himself unable to follow up his advantage from want of guns and material, and was compelled to return to Bangalore.

The disastrous events of this retreat are well known and have been described by historians. Tipú managed to obtain swift intelligence of all our proceedings, while our knowledge of his movements was almost a blank. Our battery train had to be buried. The heavy baggage was abandoned, and the sick and wounded had to be transported on horses borrowed from the native cavalry. Little or nothing was effected in the course of the same year, and Cornwallis wrote to his son, Lord Brome, that he was growing old and rheumatic and had lost all spirit. He had hopes however of bringing Tipú to terms either by negotiation or by an attack on his capital, and he did not think of leaving India before January, 1793. At the same time the Governor-General expressed his amazement, in a letter to his brother the Bishop of Lichfield, that any man of common sense could have ever imagined that the war could be avoided. It was indeed, to use his expression to Henry Dundas, 'an absolute and cruel necessity.' And it is not surprising to read that the attack made by the Opposition in both Houses, on the Mysore War, was not only a complete failure, but that it was really converted into a vote of approbation.

Towards the close of 1791 warlike operations were resumed with some vigour. The fortress of Sevendroog or Savandrúg, described by Colonel Yule as 'a remarkable double-hill fort in Mysore, standing on a two-topped, bare, rock of granite,' and long thought impregnable either by battery or escalade, was taken in the end of September. The capture of three other forts followed. The British Army had been reinforced. The native merchants collected ample stores of grain, and with the aid of a considerable army under the son of the Nizám and a small contingent of Maráthás, Cornwallis carried the fortified camp of the enemy in a night attack in which he himself was wounded, forced Tipú to evacuate all his posts to the north of the river Cauvery, and was at last in a position to lay siege to the town. The final overthrow of the Muhammadan usurper was reserved for a statesman who, gifted with remarkable energy and foresight, found India in a better state of preparation, and was aided by officers and diplomatists of the very first rank. But the termination of the two campaigns of Cornwallis is entitled to be termed a real success.

The native allies who, it was afterwards ascertained, had been in secret communication with Tipú, were content to leave protracted negotiations for peace in the hands of the English soldier and statesman. Some territory was ceded to us. A considerable sum was exacted as a fine, and the two eldest sons of Tipú were brought to the tent of the Governor-General and delivered over to him as hostages for the future. A well-known old print of this imposing ceremony is still to be found in country houses in England.

A link with the past history of Mysore was long furnished by the third son of Tipú, Prince Ghulám Muhammad, who, younger than his brothers the hostages, survived down to our own times,—a loyal, hospitable, and peaceful subject, residing in the neighbourhood of Alipur, who on two separate occasions paid a visit to England. Many Englishmen have a pleasant recollection of the old Prince's hospitality; his entertainment of Viceroys at his residence; and his black horse with a long tail that swept the ground, as he took his leisurely morning canter round the race-course of Calcutta.

Some other incidents in the foreign policy of Cornwallis's administration may be briefly noticed. Sindhia was informed, through the Resident, Major Palmer, that the Governor-General would be ready to interpose with his good offices and advice, and to adjust differences between Gwalior and the Vizir of Oudh. But the Maráthá ruler was warned at the same time that any insult offered or injury done to the Vizir or his subjects would be looked on as offered to the subjects of the Company. Though the time had not perhaps arrived for the open assertion of our position as the Paramount Power in India, the above language was suited to the occasion, and would not have been unworthy of Wellesley himself.

The succession to the Ráj of Tanjore occupied a good deal of attention. The Government at first supported the claims of Amír Singh who was in possession. On further consideration however, and especially on a letter from the celebrated missionary Schwartz, this decision was altered. Sarfijí, the adopted son of the deceased Rájá, was placed on the throne. Steps were taken to induce the Nawáb of the Karnatic to liquidate his debts and observe the stipulations of treaties; but they had not much effect, and the solution of this difficulty was also reserved for Wellesley. Captain Kirkpatrick, a very distinguished political officer, was dispatched on a mission to Nepál, where he was kindly received by the Regent, uncle of the Rájá, in spite of the strong opposition of a party of nobles who looked with suspicion on commercial treaties and European intercourse. Indeed, owing to the extensive jealousy of the king and the ministers of Nepál in each successive generation, we have scarcely made any real progress in what is termed the opening up of that kingdom to British commercial enterprise since the mission sent by Cornwallis.

With the exception of the campaigns against Tipú, the government of Cornwallis may be said to have been one of peace. The reduction of Pondicherry was one of his last acts, accomplished by a combined naval and military force. After a few discharges from our batteries the town capitulated. And this was of course followed by the temporary cession of all the other French settlements and factories in India.

It is now a pleasing task, after this brief recapitulation of the political and military events which Cornwallis directed, or in which he took a prominent part, to turn to the measures of internal reform which entitle him to rank as one of those English statesmen who have based our supremacy in India on a solid foundation, and have civilised, disciplined, and improved vast provinces acquired either by conquest or by cession. In reviewing these subjects the first place will be given to the Settlement of the Land Revenue. Under every respectable government, Hindu, Muhammadan, or foreign, the adjustment of the Land Tax has always been one of the primary objects to be attained. The due exaction of the revenue or the Land Tax has been considered the right of every *de facto* government from time immemorial, whether this power were exercised by a mighty monarch like Asoka or Akbar over splendid provinces, or by some petty Rájá with a hill fort and a few square miles of jungle streaked with cultivation. With the more enlightened rulers, such as Akbar or Sher Sháh, the due assessment of the revenue and the equitable division of the produce between the cultivator or the village community and the superior landlord, has always been a paramount duty. When we acquired the Diwání of Bengal in 1765, our first object was to realise the revenue by annual or quinquennial assessments.

Later acquisitions have impressed on our administrators the necessity of fixing the Government share of the produce on more definite principles, of collecting it by easy processes, of ascertaining the rights and interests of all classes from the superior landlord or tenant-proprietor down to the tenant-at-will, and of stereotyping these rights by a permanent and trustworthy record. It has been justly remarked that until the Land Revenue has been fixed and the Settlement concluded no other improvement should be attempted, or, if attempted, would be likely to succeed. It is vain to look for contentment and acquiescence whether in a foreign or an indigenous rule, or to set about any of those moral and material works which denote progress and civilisation, until the mass of the agriculturists know for certain in what proportions, at what periods of the year, at what places, and under what conditions or guarantees, they are to contribute to the Exchequer that portion of the harvest which they admit to be its due. No one in India, except under a special grant of exemption from the ruling power, has ever imagined that he could hold his Táluk or his allotment without paying something for it.

All these considerations were not so fully appreciated by the servants of the East India Company under Warren Hastings and Cornwallis as they have been since. But even then the collection of the revenue had been for twenty years the first and chief care of the merchants and writers who found themselves called from the desk and the counting-house to preside at the local treasury and to replenish it with contributions from a huge district. After the second administration of Lord Clive we, of course, began regularly to collect the share of the Government, and in some sense to govern the country. At first Englishmen were employed, and they soon felt the need of native collectors and subordinates. Then supervisors were appointed over the collectors. Next came local Councils at Patná, Dacca, and Murshidábád; and at last there was formed a Board of Revenue of which the President of the Council, and ultimately Lord Cornwallis as Governor-General, became a member.

The assessments were made for five years at one period, and for one year at another. The Collectors were paid by salaries and by commission, the former moderate and the latter very large. Abuses prevailed as much in the collection of the revenue due to the Government as in the realisation of the rents due to Zamíndárs. It was the object of Cornwallis almost from the moment of his arrival, to enquire into these abuses, to redress grievances, and to provide for the contentment of the cultivating community, the security of the Zamíndárs, and the interests of the East India Company, by one equitable and consistent code and system. With this object the Governor-

General judiciously sought assistance from the men best able to supply it. It would have been unreasonable for Cornwallis or for the historian of that period to expect in Collectors suddenly placed over large districts in Bengal, a minute, accurate, and diversified acquaintance with tenures, village customs, rights, responsibilities, qualities of soils, and value of produce.

Still, it is not to be imagined that some of the older Company's servants were destitute of all agricultural and revenue knowledge. In Mr. Law and in Mr. Brooke, the father of Rájá Brooke of Borneo, the Governor-General found two highly qualified and experienced officers. The celebrated *Analysis of the Finances of Bengal*, by Mr. James Grant, contains an enormous mass of information, though the conclusions are often unsound and the deductions untrustworthy. But in Mr. Shore, afterwards Lord Teignmouth, the Governor-General found a subordinate and a colleague whose understanding of the revenue and rent system of Bengal and Behar was accurate, extensive, and profound. Shore's Minutes are copious, and one, of June 1789, extends to 562 paragraphs, and covers nearly ninety pages of close print. No one could have written it who had not completely mastered the past history and present condition of the Province.

Many of Shore's observations, deductions, and reasons are as just and unimpeachable at this hour as they were when written just a century ago. His remarks on native character and proclivities are pertinent at this very day. No one can pretend to understand the origin of the Bengal Zamíndárí system who has not carefully studied this text-book on the subject. The diction is clear and perspicuous, in spite of the inevitable introduction of local phrases and terms; and in handsome language the Governor-General more than once acknowledged his obligations to the writer of these treatises, as they may fairly be termed, though he differed from Shore on more than one important point.

There has been, at various times, a good deal of discussion amongst able Anglo-Indian experts as to the precise position and rights of those whom in the Lower Provinces we have termed Zamíndárs. It is the opinion of some very competent authorities that these Zamíndárs were originally of various kinds. Sometimes they were mere agents nominated for short periods who had bid for the privilege of collecting and paying the Government dues. A very notable example of this class may be found in the *Lives of the Lindsays.* The Hon. Robert Lindsay, a servant of the East India Company, finding that one Gangá Govind, a native collector, was unequal to the collection of the revenue of the district of Sylhet, himself came forward and tendered for the right to collect, though he was opposed by the Council of Dacca. His offer was accepted by Warren Hastings, and in this way, aided by the monopoly of catching elephants and supplying the bázárs of Calcutta with oranges and lime, he legitimately acquired a large fortune. In those days such a proceeding was perfectly honourable and fair.

In other instances the native tax-collector, employed at first by the Muhammadan Nawáb of Dacca and Murshidábád, was enabled to hand over the same privilege to his son or successor, and as the office thus had a tendency to become hereditary, it was in theory associated with vested rights. But it was often found to be sound policy to entrust the collection of the revenue to the representatives of the old landed aristocracy of Bengal, and Shore particularly mentions that at the time of the acquisition of the Provinces of Bengal and Behar, one million of revenue was contributed by the Zamíndárís of the Rájás of Bardwán, Rájsháhí, Dinápur, Nadiyá, Bírbhúm, Bishnupur, and Jessor. To this day some of their representatives are in the enjoyment of fine estates. Bardwán is the largest and most flourishing, but Nadiyá or Nuddea and Jessor are in the hands of the descendants of Shore's Rájás. By Rájsháhí is meant Nattor, an estate now very much reduced in size and wealth. The Zamíndárs of Bírbhúm and Bishnupur are sunk almost to destitution, owing to mismanagement, the dishonesty of servants, litigation, and general incapacity. In 1789 it was assumed that we were to make the Settlement with the Zamíndárs, who by descent, prescription, or privilege and use, had been in the habit of collecting rents from hundreds and thousands of cultivators, and accounting to Government for its proper share or revenue.

It has been asserted at several epochs that as Cornwallis declared the Zamíndárs, with whom his Settlement was made, to be the 'proprietors of the soil,' and assured to them in his own language 'the possession of their lands,' and the profits arising from the improvement thereof, he intended to vest, and did vest them, with an absolute and exclusive right of ownership as we understand that term in England. But this is by no means the case. It is quite clear from the language of his Minutes and Letters, as well as from his legislation, that he only recognised in them a limited and not an absolute proprietorship; that he clearly perceived and was prepared to protect the rights and interests of other parties in the soil; and that the terms in which he speaks of Zamíndárs as proprietors must be taken in the Oriental and not in the English sense.

He could not practically override what for centuries had been the common law of the country. Sir George Campbell, who has the advantage of familiarity with land tenures in the Punjab, in the Upper Provinces, in Oudh, and in Bengal, pointed out some years ago that land in India was a possession in which two and more parties had very distinct, separate, and permanent interests; and that much of the confused and erroneous language applied to the subject had arisen from overlooking and disregarding this elementary fact. Those public servants who either took part in the remediary legislation of 1859 or who, previous to that date, in administering the revenue and the land laws of the Lower Provinces, endeavoured to see that the Ryot had fair play, and who insisted on the limited rights of the Zamíndár, may be certain that this latter view found favour with John Herbert Harington, author of the well-known *Analysis.* His work, published between 1815 and 1821, has long been out of print, and of course many of the Statutes, analysed and explained with wonderful clearness and precision, have been supplanted by later and better laws. But if any student of past times, or civil servant now employed in the Lower Provinces, wishes to understand thoroughly the gradual introduction of our administrative system, the terrible legacies of Muhammadan Viceroys, the difficulties encountered in the collection of the revenue and the establishment of law and order, he will study Harington's *Analysis.*

That work is for Indian legislation what Coke on Littleton is for English law. Part of Vol. III. which treats of the Land Revenue is enlivened by a controversy with Colonel Wilks who, while writing his *Historical Sketches of the South of India,* a book of much value, seemed to have completely misunderstood the Zamíndárí tenures of Bengal. What appeared to Colonel Wilks 'an inextricable puzzle,' is simplified and made clear by Harington. He began by quoting

Shore to the effect 'that the most cursory observation shows the situation of things in this country to be singularly confused. The relation of a Zamíndár to Government, and of a Ryot to a Zamíndár, is neither that of a proprietor nor a vassal, but a compound of both. The former performs acts of authority unconnected with proprietary right: the latter has rights without real property. And the property of the one and the rights of the other are in a great measure held at discretion. Such was the system which we found, and which we have been under the necessity of adopting. Much time, I fear, will elapse before we can establish a system perfectly consistent in all its parts, and before we can reduce the compound relation of a Zamíndár to Government, and of a Ryot to a Zamíndár, to the simple principles of landlord and tenant.' Then Harington himself goes on to say that this was the principal source of all the confusion which had been introduced into the discussions about Indian landed tenures. 'It is by attempting to assimilate the complicated system which we found in this country, with the simple principles of landlord and tenant in our own, and especially in applying to the Indian system terms of appropriate and familiar signification which do not without considerable limitation properly belong to it, that much, if not all, of the perplexity ascribed to the subject has arisen.' He follows this up by a definition of the Zamíndár as we found him, which for well-balanced antithesis, recognition of rights followed by language of positive limitation, and fair solution of perplexing contradictions, has probably not been surpassed in any Minute, State Paper, or Proclamation on the subject.

'The Zamíndár appears to be a Landholder of a peculiar description, not definable by any single term in our language. A receiver of the territorial Revenue of the State from the Ryots and other under-tenants of the land: allowed to succeed to his Zamíndárí by inheritance, yet in general required to take out a renewal of his title from the Sovereign, or his representative, on payment of a *peshkash* or fine of investiture to the Emperor, and a *nazaráná* or present to his provincial delegate the Názim: permitted to transfer his Zamíndárí by sale or gift, yet commonly expected to obtain previous special permission: privileged to be generally the annual contractor for the public revenue receivable from his Zamíndárí, yet set aside with a limited provision in land or money, whenever it was the pleasure of the Government to collect the rents by separate agency or to assign them temporarily or permanently by the grant of a Jaghír or Altamghá; authorized in Bengal since the early part of the present century to apportion to the Parganás, villages, and lesser divisions of land within his Zamíndárí, the *abwábs* or cesses imposed by the Subahdar, usually in some proportion to the Standard Assessment of the Zamíndárí established by Todar Mall, and others; yet subject to the discretionary interference of public authority, to equalize the amount assessed on particular divisions or to abolish what appeared oppressive to the Ryot: entitled to any contingent emoluments proceeding from his contract during the period of his agreement, yet bound by the laws of his tenure to deliver in a faithful account of his receipts: responsible by the same terms for keeping the peace within his jurisdiction, but apparently allowed to apprehend only and deliver over to a Musalmán magistrate for trial and punishment—this is, in abstract, my present idea of a Zamíndár under the Mughal constitution and practice.'

This was the opinion of the young revenue officer, who had been brought up in the school of Hastings, and twenty-eight years afterwards, with his ripe experience, he saw no reason to alter his language. But he then explains the changes in the Zamíndár's situation and privileges which the Permanent Settlement had introduced. Glancing at the reservation to Government of the power to legislate for the protection of dependent Tálukdárs, Ryots, and other cultivators, he remarks that the Zamíndár was now at liberty to appropriate to his own use the difference between the portion of the produce which was the right of Government, and his own private rent. This share was already estimated to be treble what it had been before 1793, and looking to this increment and advantage, Harington was prepared to recognise the Zamíndárs, Tálukdárs, and all landholders, of whatever denomination, as 'proprietors in a general sense.'

In other not unimportant particulars their position was secured and improved. Heirs and successors were no longer called on to take out a *sanad*, or deed of investiture, in ratification of their succession. They were not expected to pay the former *Peshkash* or the *Nazaráná*. No permission was needed for the sale or transfer of an estate. As long as the revenue was fully and punctually paid, the Zamíndár was no longer subject to temporary or permanent removal from the management of the Zamíndárí. As he had been relieved from the imposition of new or extra cesses, he was bound to abstain from imposing similar taxes on his Ryots. But he was no longer liable to furnish any accounts of receipts and disbursements, except when such accounts were essential to the apportionment of the Public Revenue on the division of an estate between joint-shareholders. Finally, he had been relieved of the charge of the police, and was only expected to aid the regular officials of the Government by preserving the peace and giving information of crimes and heinous offences. And as Harington had previously defined the status of a Zamíndár under the Mughal Government and during the administrations of Clive, Verelst, Cartier, and Hastings, he wound up by a definition applicable to his new position under the Cornwallis Code. He had become 'a landholder, possessing a Zamíndárí estate which is hereditable and transferable by sale, gift, or bequest: subject under all circumstances to the public assessment fixed upon it: entitled, after payment of such assessment, to appropriate any surplus rents or profits which may lawfully be receivable by him from the under-tenants of land in his Zamíndárí or from the improvement and cultivation of untenanted lands; but subject nevertheless to such rules and restrictions as are already established or may be hereafter enacted by the British Government, for securing the rights and privileges of Ryots and other under-tenants of whatever denomination, in their respective tenures; and for protecting them against undue exaction or oppression.'

Cornwallis had two very distinct objects in view. He wished to recognise the Zamíndárs as landed proprietors with the prospect of an increased rental from the cultivation of the land, and he desired that the Settlement made with them for ten years should be declared permanent and fixed for ever. Here was one of the points in which he differed from Shore, and a large part of the Minutes and State Papers of the day is taken up with long discussions on this head.

Briefly stated, Shore held that the capacities of the land had not been properly ascertained: that we had no staff of men possessed of sufficient knowledge of the vast and intricate subjects of rents, tenures, and agricultural interests; that great abuses prevailed in the levy by Zamíndárs of extra cesses from the Ryots; that it was desirable to diminish the size of vast Zamíndárís and to increase the number of small proprietors: that these ends could not be attained without time and trouble; and, in short, that before committing ourselves to an irrevocable Settlement in Perpetuity it would be prudent and politic to wait. Lord Cornwallis replied that we had not then, and should not have at the end of ten years, any staff of officials capable of entering into such minute and complicated details; that a very large portion of the Province was waste and jungle, and that a Permanent Settlement would give confidence to the Zamíndárs, increase to agriculture, and stability to Government. It is well here to dwell on a fact which of late years has been conveniently or negligently overlooked; and this is that the share of the Zamíndár was in those days reckoned at only one-tenth of his whole receipts. The remaining nine-tenths were to go to the Government. If a Zamíndár declined after a trial to engage for the collection of the revenue in any district, and another man became the collecting agent, an allowance, of ten per cent. only, was set aside for the excluded Zamíndár, and the same rule was followed in the case of minors and females. Shore anticipated that on the confirmation of the proposed assessment, the profits of the Zamíndár might reach to nearly fifteen per cent. It is not superfluous to state that while we have no absolute certainty as to the net profits of Zamíndárs at the present day, we may safely conclude that in very many cases they far exceed Shore's moderate estimate.

In another important point Shore and Cornwallis were at issue. There were certain internal duties which the Zamíndárs had been in the habit of levying. They were known as *sáyer* and *ráhdárí* or transit dues, and as taxes on goods exposed for sale in the wholesale and retail markets of the country. It is not necessary now to go into these differences at great length, though a knowledge of them may be deemed indispensable to the young civilian of the present day. The result can be shortly put. The *sáyer* duties were local and arbitrary charges levied by Zamíndárs on goods passing through their estates by land and water. The *ráhdárí* were similar in kind. This word properly means a permission or permit for goods to pass: a kind of black mail. Both kinds were formally abolished by the Laws of 1790 and 1793.

Since that date, though such dues have been occasionally levied throughout Bengal by oppressive and high-handed Zamíndárs, within the memory and cognizance of men still living, the theory has been that Zamíndárs are confined in the collection of their dues to rents of cultivated lands, to fisheries, to pasture, and to the natural yield of the jungle and forest. A little further explanation may be expedient in regard to duties levied by Zamíndárs, not on goods passing through their estates and in transit from one Zamíndárí or Parganá to another, but on goods brought and exposed to sale at certain distinct places. These are designated by Shore in language applicable to this very hour, as the Ganj, the Bázár, and the Hát. The Ganj is a wholesale market, though articles may also be retailed at such places by the smaller traders. Familiar examples of such Ganjs, which are centres of enormous traffic, are Sirájganj in Pabná, Nalchití in Bákarganj, and Náráinganj in

Dacca. A Bázár is simply an assemblage of ten, twenty, or fifty and more houses and shops for the retail of all articles of subsistence. By a *Hát* is meant a place where vegetables, fruits, and the necessaries of life are exposed for sale, generally on two special days in the week. Sometimes each permanent bázár has its bi-weekly market or *Hát*.

But quite as often a *Hát* is held in an open space where there is not a single permanent structure of any kind. On *Hát* days such places are resonant with the hum of two thousand voices of buyers and sellers. On other days the *Hát* is a lifeless, untenanted, vacant space. It is very significant when we consider the point of absolute ownership claimed for Zamíndárs, that there was a considerable amount of discussion on paper whether these Ganjs, Bázárs, and Háts should not be taken entirely away from the Zamíndárs, and separated from their estates. The opinion actually prevailed in some quarters that the rights and privileges of the Zamíndárs were to be confined to arable and pasture, to fisheries and forests alone.

In some parts of the Province, the Zamíndárs did not even claim the Ganj at all. Shore mentions the cases of men who had become proprietors of Ganj and Bázárs without any Zamíndárí rights. In the end, all three descriptions of markets were handed over to the Zamíndárs within whose estates they were found; and amongst their rights and privileges none, to this day, is more valued or often more productive, than the privilege of setting up a new *Hát* or Bázár. Indeed, down to recent times Bázárs were set up by powerful proprietors with the express object of ruining a rival and attracting his buyers and sellers; and many outrages, fights, and affrays and much litigation used to ensue from such proceedings some thirty and forty years ago.

It is no disparagement to the discernment of Cornwallis that he had not such a vivid notion of the interior of a district in Bengal and Behar as was present to the mind of Shore. But it is also clear that Cornwallis had managed to grasp successfully some of the main points in the agricultural and revenue system of the Province and that, as before stated, he did not by any means intend to hand over the whole agricultural and village community to the superior landlords to be dealt with by them on the terms of contract and under the economic laws of demand and supply. To prove this we have only to read carefully his Minutes and Regulations. He was in favour of multiplying smaller proprietors, as he was of opinion that their management was better. He conceded to some smaller *Túlukdárs* the privilege of payment of revenue direct to the Government Treasury instead of through the superior Zamíndár. Such estates in revenue phraseology were called *Huzúrí* in contradistinction to *Shikmí* Táluks.

He laid down the principle that a Zamíndár could only receive the customary or established rent, and that he had no right to dispossess any one cultivator for the sole purpose of giving his land to another. He insisted that Zamíndárs should grant *pattás* or documents specifying the amount which the Ryots were to pay 'by whatever rule or custom it may be demanded.' Every cess or 'benevolence' known as *abwáb*, imposed by the Zamíndár, was declared by Cornwallis to be a breach of his agreement and a direct violation of the established laws of the country.

He expressly reserved to Government the right to enquire into and to resume alienations of land granted for religious and secular purposes to favourites, Brahmans, astrologers, priests, and other classes: and one of the sections of the Regulation or Law in which he embodied these views contains, as has been shown, an intimation that as it was the duty of the ruling power to protect the helpless classes, the Governor-General in Council, whenever he might deem it proper, would enact such Regulations as he might think necessary for the safety and welfare of the dependent Tálukdárs, Ryots, and other cultivators of the soil. In many other ways was a limit imposed on the power of the Zamíndár. Though permitted to sell and mortgage his estates, he was not by any such transaction to endanger the realisation of the Government revenue.

Although private sales of estates were not numerous the shares of joint-proprietors had to be separated. And the separation, which at first only meant that each shareholder collected his rents by a separate agent, in the end resulted in a division of the territorial estate. It then became the duty of the Collector to see that each separate portion or cluster of villages was assessed with its proper amount of revenue. And in any private transfer or any official division of the land, the interest of Government was effectively protected by the action of the Collector. Unless this person had given his sanction to the transaction, the whole original estate was held liable for the dues of Government.

For some time subsequent to the Code of 1793 Zamíndárs were prevented by law from granting leases beyond a certain term of years and creating perpetual sub-infeudations. The Zamíndár, it has been shown, was to take the bad years with the good, and as he was liable to no enhancement, he was to expect no remission in drought or scarcity. When an estate was put up to public auction, the incoming purchaser acquired his new possession free from any fresh encumbrances created by his predecessor. And at some periods of our rule many ingenious frauds were attempted. Zamíndárs, who had received a bonus for the creation of an encumbrance or sub-infeudation, purposely allowed their estates to be put up to auction for arrears, then purchased them in the name of a dependent or third person, and tried to annul the subordinate titles which they had themselves created. This sort of proceeding had, however, very little effect on the actual tenant-proprietor or cultivator. And his position was to some extent safeguarded by a rule that the Zamíndár was not at liberty to enhance the ordinary rent without resorting to a regular civil suit. Actions to fix the rent of a Ryot or to bring it up to the standard of the Parganá or the neighbourhood became common. The judicial rent now familiar to English readers from its recent introduction into Ireland, was the law of the land in India a century ago. It has never been shown how this necessity of a resort to a judicial tribunal could be compatible with any theory of absolute and unlimited ownership.

Still, the position of the Rájá, Zamíndár, or Chaudárí during and after the administration of Cornwallis was in many respects one of power, privilege, and profit. And something must now be added in regard to what was either conferred on him by law or recognised by judicial decisions. An estate, which is often used as the English equivalent for the term Zamíndárí or Táluk, in Bengal merely denotes a certain tract of land, with boundaries loosely given or not defined at all, which is burdened with a certain specific amount of revenue. It may mean a single village, a cluster of villages, portions of several villages, or a principality as big as an English county. Each estate bears a separate number on the roll of the Collectorate and is usually described as situated in such or such a Parganá or Chaklá. In revenue phraseology the villages contained in the estate are termed *Mauzás*: a word which would not be employed by an ordinary speaker talking of the village in which he resided or to which he was bound. But whether the estate were large or small, the Zamíndár was entitled to demand his rent from every tenant: and he alone could induct new tenants into their holdings. All waste and untenanted lands were his. He might cultivate them by hired labour, which he rarely or never did, or he might induce new Ryots to settle there under his protection, build houses for themselves, clear the jungle, and break up the soil. In such instances the rent demanded was at first very small. On lands that had been long under cultivation the rent varied with the nature of the crop. There was a moderate rate for rice crops grown on the higher ground, and a heavier rate on rice in the deep land. The better kinds of produce were more heavily taxed than either of the above, such as sugar-cane, tobacco, and *pán*: and gardens and homesteads usually paid the highest of all. All plots vacated by famine, desertion, or death, *ipso facto* reverted to the Zamíndár. He was allowed to challenge the titles of all who claimed to hold small plots as Lákhiráj or rent-free, and the onus of proving a valid grant from some former authority, empowered to make such a title, was by the judicial courts always thrown on the Lákhirájdár. It was held in the case of squatters or Ryots who had never asked for or received any *pattás* or titles to their holding, that no period of time could bar the Zamíndár's claim to rent. As he was bound to pay the revenue, a demand for rent to pay it constituted a cause of action, and no amount of time in which payment had not been demanded, or had been withheld, could create a title to sit rent-free. In theory it was asserted that most Ryots could not sell or transfer their holdings without the consent of the superior landlord.

But in treating of the Ryot's position it will be shown that in this respect practice was at variance with theory. Over jungle, waste, scrub and swamp, the Zamíndár had equally clear rights. They were termed *Bankar*, or forest produce: *Jalkar*, fishery: *Phulkar*, honey and fruits: and *Thalkar*, what dropped on the ground. When the Zamíndár was minded to expend money on his Zamíndárí, his expenditure generally took the following shape. He might drain a huge swamp by cutting a channel for the overflow of its water into the nearest river. He excavated by paid labour an enormous reservoir which secured a supply of pure water for half-a-dozen villages. He constructed *ghâts* or landing-places of stone or brick on the banks of rivers or tanks. He dedicated temples and built school-houses. But he never controlled the agricultural operations of his tenants, or thought himself bound to provide them with houses or to fence their land.

It is clear that Cornwallis did not fully comprehend the custom of the country in regard to the spread of cultivation. In the first and most important of his Regulations he expresses a hope that the Zamíndárs would exert themselves to cultivate their lands, and would improve their respective estates, and he assures them that they would enjoy exclusively the fruits of their own industry without any fear that the demands of Government would be augmented in consequence of any such increase of cultivation and enhanced value of landed property. From the use of the above phrases we can only conceive the ideal or typical Zàmíndár whom Cornwallis had in his mind, to be identical with what in England we should call an improving landlord: one who expends capital in planting trees where corn will not grow with profit, in making hedges, clearing out ditches, draining wet lands, and erecting model cottages of the most approved type. Now it has been already shown that the Zamíndár in almost every district did spend considerable sums in digging tanks, building temples and *ghâts*, and cutting canals. But he never spent a farthing on drains, cottages, breaking up jungle and waste land, or in introducing the higher and more lucrative kinds of cultivation on any holding within his estate. The whole of this burden fell on the Ryot.

It is true that a Zamíndár gave to the Ryot whom he inducted into a plot of ground, the countenance which was at all times indispensable in such a country as India. He was occasionally, to such tenants, a refuge from the tyranny and encroachment of a rival landholder. But it was the mattock and axe of the Ryot and the exercise of the Ryot's thews and sinews that cut down the jungle and cleared the waste. He worked, as it were, for himself under the Zamíndár's shadow. The new ground which he broke up without the slightest help from the superior landlord and his agents, was frequently assessed for some years at a very low rate. It might be a half or a quarter of the usual rental, or a mere nominal rate for the first twelvemonth. Sometimes, from the negligence or the indifference of the local manager, a holding might escape taxation for several seasons, or the Ryot might take in additional land beyond the amount specified in his deed of induction. But whatever might be the fate of the Ryot, and whether his Zamíndár was careless or precise in the assessment and exaction of rent, it is indisputable that all over Bengal the Zamíndár looked on placidly while the tenant-proprietor and the Ryot burnt the jungle grass, broke up the clay soil, sowed the rice, and introduced gradually the more valuable products.

It is not necessary in accepting these facts, to censure the Zamíndárs as a class for not at once filling the exact position of improving landlords which Cornwallis had anticipated. The custom of the country from the earliest times was for the Ryot to toil under the Zamíndár's protection. But the Zamíndár had often private lands or lands in his own occupation, termed in the phraseology of the day *Nij-jot* and *Khás Khámár*; and he was not in the habit, in respect of such plots, of showing the tenantry how the yield of the land could be increased by manure, or how on the various levels the cereals, the date-tree, the *jute*, the tobacco-plant or the sugar-cane, could be sown and grown with profit. Practically in these cases his own servants or hired labourers cultivated the Khás lands and produced very indifferent results. The main object of the Zamíndárs, for years after 1793, was to induct Ryots into waste and culturable lands, as population increased and as more space and new villages were required to meet the wants of a growing community.

It was one of the cardinal points of the new Settlement that Government on the one hand would not impose any additional taxation on any lands within the supposed area of any estate which had been cleared and cultivated, or on account of any luxuriant harvest in any one year. On the other hand, the Zamíndár was not to expect remissions or suspensions of the revenue when his lands suffered from drought, inundation, or other calamity of the season. He was bound to take the lean and the fat years together and to make the best of both. If he failed in the punctual discharge of his obligations to the State, no excuse could be accepted. His estate, or a portion sufficient to make good the arrears due, would be put up to auction peremptorily and sold to the highest bidder. He was not allowed to plead the default or incapacity of a shareholder, though he could always protect his own interests by paying up the defaulter's portion, and recovering his payments by means of a civil action. The provisions of the Sale Law were stringent, but they were an improvement on the ancient mode of compelling payment by the confinement of the defaulter or by his corporal punishment. And a sure and certain spread of cultivation was the natural consequence of the cessation of Muhammadan oppression and Maráthá raids. The operations of nature in that region were always effected on a gigantic scale. If the drought was of long continuance or the inundations widespreading and calamitous, as was often the case in Central and Eastern Bengal, the silt deposited by the overflowing waters elevated and fertilised the soil. The reed and the bulrush made way for the rice crop. The jungle retreated before the axe and the plough. The swamp became firm land. And around new villages and hamlets there sprang up fruit trees, bamboos, and a rich and artificial vegetation almost as dense as the primeval forest which it had displaced. In all this there was an increase to the profits of the Zamíndár.

The documents which he was expected to give to Ryots, new or old, were known as *pattás,* and the Ryot was bound to hand in exchange for the same what was termed a *kabúliyat* or acceptance. These two terms have very often, in judicial decisions, formal reports, and other documents, been loosely denominated as leases and their counterparts. In truth the *pattá* of an ordinary Ryot has no resemblance to an English lease. No term of years is specified. There are stipulations to the effect that the Ryot is not to withhold his rent or fail in payment on the plea of drought or inundation, death or desertion of joint-shareholders, or tenants-at-will without occupancy rights.

Timber and fruit trees were not to be cut down. Not that they had been planted by the hand of the Zamíndár, but because by their destruction the value of the holding was lessened. Similarly, if a substantial tenant wished to excavate a tank, the Zamíndár might, if he chose, put in an objection on the ground that any diminution of the culturable or cultivated area diminished the security for rent. As a matter of fact, however, such objections were comparatively rare. Many of the Bengal villages suffer from a redundancy of reservoirs not sufficiently deep and not always kept in proper repair. These rights and privileges were coupled with certain liabilities and duties. The Zamíndár was bound to provide means to carry the post on what we should call cross-country roads. This postal service rarely went beyond the transmission of heavy police reports. Besides his obligation to assist the police, the Zamíndár was bound to prevent the illicit manufacture of salt and the unauthorised cultivation of the poppy, inasmuch as Government retained the monopoly of opium and salt. The Zamíndár was also credited with the maintenance and pay of the village watchmen. But for many years the postal service between police stations and the magistrate's court, as well as the Chaukidárí or village watch system, was on a most unsatisfactory footing.

If some of the above responsibilities were occasionally inconvenient and irksome, they could also be turned into instruments of power and oppression in the hands of energetic landlords who could afford to have good legal advice and who were well served by active agents and retainers. While inexperienced and indifferent Zamíndárs were cheated by their servants, baffled by combinations of Ryots, and driven to the expedient of creating sub-infeudations which left them rent-chargers on their own estates; others, with energy and intelligence and without scruples, managed to avail themselves of every clause and section of the law, and to convert statutory liabilities into sources of profit. They sent their agents to measure holding after holding, and levied rents on all lands in excess of the *pattá*, as they had a perfect right to do. They sued substantial Ryots for enhanced rents, in order to exact the rates leviable by common custom on the better products. In spite of repeated prohibitions, legal and executive, they demanded and received extra cesses known as *abwábs* at every remarkable incident in their lives: the birth of a son, the marriage of a daughter, the dedication of a temple, the erection of a school, the building of a ghát, the march of a high official through the district, the receipt of a title or a dress of honour from the Government, the termination of a great lawsuit, or any other propitious or unpropitious event: and it may certainly be conceded that, if not in the exact position of an English landlord, the Zamíndár was by Lord Cornwallis raised from an uncertain to a well-defined place, and to one of emolument, privilege, and power. It could no longer be altered at the caprice of some wayward autocrat ruling at Dacca or Murshidábád. It was stamped with the seal of a foreign power whose representatives were known to be men of their word. It could only be forfeited by incapacity or wilful default. And finally the Zamíndár might raise money on his estate, mortgage and sell it, and transmit it to his heirs and successors, increased in value, unimpeachable in title, and unaffected by any rise in price or any further claims of the State.

In treating of the rights, interests, and position of the Ryot, it would be impossible, in the limits of this memoir, to describe the various Ryotty tenures to be found in the Provinces to which the Perpetual Settlement was applied. Many which bear different titles in different districts of the Lower Provinces, are in substance and reality almost identical. In some cases the distinctions are more apparent than solid; and certainly at various epochs, when the position and claims of the Ryots have been investigated, it has generally been found possible to class them under three great divisions. Important but comparatively few in number, as has been often pointed out, are the tenants who hold land at rates positively fixed before the Perpetual Settlement, or at rates never enhanced or varied since that date. These valuable tenures are commonly denominated *istimrárí*, or *mukarrarí*, and to these titles there is often appended the word *maurúsí*, or hereditary. No claim for enhancement can affect a valid title of this kind.

Next in the scale are resident Ryots, who, though not holding nor claiming to hold at unchangeable rates, have been considered to have a right to retain their tenures as long as they pay their rents, and against whom claims for enhancement must be urged and proved by the formal process of a regular civil suit. These have a sort of proprietary right: they form a very considerable and important class; and much discussion and litigation have ensued in regard to individual cases as well as to the claims of the whole body. The third and last class is that of cultivators without any rights of occupancy. These latter are very often the sub-tenants of tenant-proprietors, and as such are variously known as *shikmí*, *kurfa*, or *koljána* Ryots. These terms are almost identical and are perfectly well understood. Of course this class is to be found on large and small estates holding directly under the Zamíndár or Tálukdár.

For all practical purposes it would not be difficult to assign to tenants in any part of the Lower Provinces a place in one or other of the above categories. They hold either from 1793 or possibly before it, at an unchanged and unchangeable rate. Or they have a right of occupancy and cannot legally be evicted, though by a civil action their rates may be brought up to the scale prevalent in the Parganá in which they reside, or in the neighbouring villages. Or they are sub-tenants or tenants without rights of occupancy, and it may be conceded that in recent times their rents have been the subject of contract. Practically in the first half of this century their rates were settled by custom and mutual understanding.

It is essential to lay stress on the occupancy right because doubts have been thrown on its existence, and attempts have been made in the interest of the Zamíndárs to prove that if ever in existence, it had perished or was so faint as not to merit legal recognition. But it is far more correct to say that if the right was not recognised by statute till long after the time of Cornwallis, it was an article of firm belief held by a large proportion of the peasantry. Payment of rent is almost everywhere in India regarded as an obligation from which no cultivator can escape. A regular discharge of this obligation is often put forward as a mark of respectability. Failure or refusal to pay would stamp the recusant as a *badmáish* or bad character. But then this admitted obligation was balanced, in the mind of a large number of cultivators, by the comforting reflection that there could be no capricious eviction of those who paid.

In many districts of Bengal the occupancy Ryot has always played an important part in the spread of cultivation and the improvement of agriculture. He may be known by various denominations. He is the *jotdár* or the *Gánthidár* or the *Khúd-Kásht* Ryot. This last term signifies a tenant whose homestead and holding are in one and the same village. In many instances his family has lived in the same place for generations. He has erected two, three, and four houses, neatly built of bamboos and wattles, well thatched, with a verandah on more than one side, and the whole raised on a firm foundation of well-beaten clay. The space between the houses ensures privacy. The courtyard and the dwellings are scrupulously clean. They are shaded by fine trees, and the garden adjoining the house is dense with foliage and heavy with fruit. Many of this class, if not rich, are independent and comfortable, and in spite of the antagonism between Zamíndár and Ryot, which has been the normal state of parts of the country for some two or three generations, many more of this useful class have maintained their position than is often supposed. It is the result of a community of interest on the part of the cultivating castes, of a passionate attachment to the native village and the ancestral homestead, and of the popular and well-founded belief that the Zamíndár had at no period the power, and not often the will, to resort to evictions. And instances of abuse of power and of a disregard and defiance of law, police, and magistrates, for particular objects, are no proof of any deliberate intention to override what may be termed the common law of the country.

Left to himself in many matters, the Ryot was his own master in all the processes of agriculture and cropping. No Zamíndár ever dreamt of insisting on rotation of crops, consumption of straw on the spot, or any of those familiar conditions which tenants in other countries holding under contracts are compelled to accept. The tenant-proprietor and even the non-occupancy Ryot, erects his own dwelling-house, finds his own materials, puts up his slender fences, cuts the channel to conduct superfluous water from his own plot to his neighbour's, maintains the small embankments of earth that serve for communication over the plain as well as for boundaries of holdings, expends time and money on the higher and more remunerative species of produce, and in short makes the most of his land without advice, direction, or hindrance from the superior landlord. These are distinct and irrefragable proofs of a permanent interest in the land, and yet they are perfectly compatible with the existence of rights and privileges of others. It has been said in a previous part of the memoir that the Ryot was expected to notify to his superior any sale or transfer of his own interest. But that duty, though admitted in theory, was frequently disregarded in practice It is absolutely certain that the *jot* or *jamma* of a Ryot had a market value of its own. It was often put up to public auction in satisfaction of a decree of court, and was bid for and bought by purchasers without the least reference to the Zamíndár. And almost as often, holdings changed hands by private agreement.

Sometimes a Ryot parted with his holding and was reinstated as a mere cultivator. Sometimes he conveyed it to his own Zamíndár, and sometimes again the Zamíndár was in the habit of buying holdings situated within the estate of a neighbour and a rival, for purposes of intimidation, annoyance, and revenge. In other cases the Ryot's holdings have been purchased openly and fairly, and with a perfectly lawful object, by the Zamíndár himself. If the Zamíndár had no spare land of a requisite class, and wished for a small plot on which to lay out a garden, build a temple, or excavate a tank, he was forced to bargain with his own Ryot to cede land for the purpose.

He would not be supported by law, custom, or public opinion in forcibly demanding a cession of the Ryot's land without compensation or equivalent. In England any such requirement of the superior landlord would easily be met, at the end of an annual or periodical lease, by the retention of a farm or any portion of a farm in the hands of the owner. But Cornwallis did not find, and he did not introduce, any system of periodical leases or of rents based on contract.

Some of the Ryot's rights and customs may at first sight appear conflicting and irreconcilable. But they are in reality quite capable of distinct identification and of severance.

Zamíndárs, on the one hand, usually know perfectly well how far they can assert their privileges, and when they will be resisted or upheld by the law; and Ryots, on the other, though pressed for rents, harshly treated by agents, and compelled to supply additional funds for the necessities and the caprices of the landlord, have often successfully met violence by artifice, learnt in their turn the power of combination for safety, and held their ground till their position was defined, stereotyped by statute, and eventually upheld in the courts of law.

CHAPTER III

PRINCIPLES AND RESULTS

SOME additional remarks on the apparent conflict of landlords' and tenants' rights and duties will be found in the chapter giving a summary of the legislation rendered necessary as a corollary to the Perpetual Settlement. But a few more words may now be said as to the other effects of that measure on the condition of the country, and as to its fulfilment or non-fulfilment of the expectations of its author. The opinions of the press on the policy of the measure are not without their value. The editor of the *Calcutta Gazette* on the 21st of May, 1789, expressed his satisfaction at the announcement that, in September of that year, the revenue of the Behar province would be fixed in perpetuity. 'We venture to observe,' he said, 'that the main principles admit a positive right of property in the landholders in opposition to a system which has been maintained by some, that the Zamíndárs and Tálukdárs are public officers only, and that the Sovereign is the real proprietor of the lands, which he leases out as landlord instead of levying a tax on them as ruler. The most important benefits may be expected from this decision. The proprietor, stimulated by self-interest, will improve his estate to the utmost of his ability, without apprehension of losing the fruits of his improvements from an increase in his payments to Government; and without fear of dispossession from the management of another being more likely to augment the produce of his lands to the State.' About the same time the editor observed that a Settlement of the revenues of this country for a long term of years would produce greater advantages than those which had been inferred. 'By allowing a certain return to industry, free from any deduction for the public tax, it is probable that extensive plans of improvement would be undertaken, agriculture increase, and commerce flourish. The landlord, secure in the enjoyment of his profits, would be averse to rack-rent his under-tenants, and these in a country where cultivators, not employers, are sought for, would be interested in encouraging the peasantry. In short, a permanent system promises ease to the lower order of subjects, opulence to the middle and higher ranks, and a punctual realisation of the tax of Government.'

The editor also stated that the Governor-General had come to the important resolution of taking into the immediate charge of Government the collection of the Ganj, Bázár, Hát, and other duties generally denominated Sáyer, both in the estates paying revenue and in the Altamghá, Aima, Jágírs, and other Lákhiráj or rent-free tenures. It has been already shown that though the above project was discussed and considered, the Ganjes, Bázárs, and Háts were left as appendages to the Zamíndárís. The Sáyer or transit dues were, however, abolished.

The editorial written after the Proclamation of the Perpetual Settlement for the three Provinces is, in its way, so remarkable that it has been thought proper to reproduce it in its entirety. It will be recollected that the Indian press was then in its infancy, and that newspapers were not free to discuss every political event. The remarks on a novel and important measure, as it appeared to a writer who, though he cannot be pronounced altogether independent, had yet undertaken to acquaint the community with the views and intentions of Government, will not be without their interest. They are somewhat analogous to the first criticisms on the appearance of a great historical work or a poem destined to become famous. The editorial of the 9th of May, 1793, is as follows:—

'We have great pleasure in announcing to the public an event which immediately concerns the native landholders, and is certainly an object of the greatest political importance to the welfare of these provinces. The circumstance we mention is a proclamation issued by the Governor-General in Council, declaring that the *Jamma* which has been assessed on the lands of the different description of proprietors in Bengal, Behar and Orissa, under the Regulations for the

Decennial Settlement of the public revenue, is from henceforth fixed for ever.

'To enter into a detail of the advantages that will, in all probability, be derived from the various articles of this proclamation, by confirming the claims of all ranks of proprietors, and abolishing many inferior duties, would lead into a very wide field, which we could but imperfectly explore; but the great purpose of it, the permanent settlement of the land-tax, we consider as involving so much political truth with practical benefit, that we cannot pass it over without endeavouring to illustrate what it is impossible not to admire.

'It has frequently been a subject of controversy among philosophers and financiers, whether the taxation of land should be fixed according to a certain valuation, not afterwards to be altered, or formed on a scale which varies with each variation of the real rent of the land, and rises or falls with the improvement or declension of its cultivation. Government has, on the present occasion, adopted the former system; and we think, however specious the latter may appear, it is founded on a mistaken principle, as it in argument supposes that considerable improvements will arise, while in fact it at the same moment throws the strongest check upon every species of improvement and industry; namely, that the Government, which bears no part in the expense, shall bear away a share of the profits of improvement.

'Under the former system of land-tax, the revenue is rendered certain to the Government as well as to the Individual, and nothing is left to the arbitrary disposal of the one, or the evasion and dishonesty of the other; at the same time the strongest inducement is held out to the proprietor to improve the value of his estate, for as that is improved, not only his general comfort and wealth are increasing, but the very tax itself is rendered more light by bearing a smaller proportion to the increased value and produce. Nor is Government excluded from sharing in these advantages, though in a less immediate way, for the immediate consequence of an increase of produce is an increase of the population of the country, whose industry returns again to the fields, or overflows into the manufactories which work upon their productions.

'Such are the effects which must result from the humane and wise principles announced by this proclamation, which opens a new era in the history of our Government in the East, and must be considered by the natives as the greatest blessing conferred on them for many ages.

'During the period of the Muhammadan Government, the assessment on land was subject to numerous and arbitrary impositions; that assessment, since the English have been in possession of these Provinces, has been variously levied and frequently augmented; the evil effects of this desultory system were severely felt; they will now have been completely remedied; the Decennial Settlement placed the revenue on the equitable footing of a fixed unalterable assessment provisionally, until the Court of Directors should give their approbation to it. That Settlement is now confirmed for ever.

'With regard to the amount of the *jamma*, its moderation is sufficiently proved by the complete payment of the revenue last year to Government, except in two Zamíndárís, not only without a balance, but with the additional collection of former suspensions.

'By these measures a permanent revenue is secured to Government, property to individuals, and a prospect of wealth and happiness is opened to the natives co-extensive with the industry and capital they shall think fit to employ in the cultivation and improvement of their lands.'

It will be seen from the above that the editor shared in the delusion that the proprietors would themselves expend capital in improving their estates. His anticipations of industrial enterprise and manufactories were certainly a little premature. But no exception can be taken to the remark that the Proclamation was the commencement of a new era, and that it was in striking contrast to the system adopted by Muhammadan Viceroys, and to a certain extent by the Anglo-Indian Government for more than twenty years. As Cornwallis had anticipated, an immediate impulse was given to cultivation. Invasions of Maghs from Arakan, common in the sixteenth century, and the Maráthá raids of the earlier part of the eighteenth century, had come to an end.

The agriculturists of Bengal had thus been secured against robbery from without before the time of Cornwallis. They were now in a position to increase and multiply, to found villages in spots tenanted only by the wild boar, the deer, and the tiger, and they had only to contend with the exaction and rapacity of their own countrymen. There was also the semblance and outward show of executive authority, and the people began dimly to discern that their lives and properties were no longer held under the good-will and caprice of irresponsible despots.

At any rate it is quite certain that, aided by natural agencies, the agriculturists soon began to lessen the area of uncultivated and forest land and to make inroads on the swamps. The copious rainfall, and the overflow of many of the network of rivers which find their way into the Bay of Bengal, have had the effect of gradually raising the level of the soil, silting up the marsh, and replacing the fish-weir and the net of the fowler by the plough. The author of this memoir himself had the advantage of hearing from the mouth of a civil servant[1] who began his career in 1793 and ended it in 1845, after more than fifty years of continuous service on the Bengal establishment, the opinion which was held by some very competent judges of the paramount necessity of a permanent assessment at the time of the famous Proclamation. It was, he said, such as to leave the Governor-General hardly any option at all. There was difficulty in some districts in getting well-qualified persons to engage for the realisation of the public revenue.

There was even greater difficulty in keeping them to their engagements. Whole districts, easily reclaimable, were covered with grass jungle and reeds. In others, the primeval forest of Sal and other timber trees had scarcely been touched by the axe. On many of the public roads, or rather on the wretched

[1] The late Mr. James Pattle, senior member of the Board of Revenue for many years, to his death in September, 1845.

tracks of communication impassable for wheeled carriages for at least five months in the year, the runners who conveyed the post were constantly carried off by tigers. There was plausibility in the argument that without a guarantee against any increase to the land-tax, the Zamíndárí system, if not doomed to failure, would never be a success. But it is admitted that the judgment of posterity has endorsed the wiser opinion of Shore. Many of the advantages of a Perpetual Settlement might have been equally attainable by a Settlement for a long term of years. It is only fair, in judging Cornwallis, to take into consideration the stubborn difficulties which he had to face.

Many of the subsidiary measures, executive and legislative, necessary for the complete success of the measure, were not immediately carried out. Some indeed were unaccountably and unwarrantably delayed. A summary of them will be given in the chapter descriptive of subsequent legislation. They included the resumption of invalid rent-free tenures: the creation of facilities for the recovery of rent by summary process; and the protection of the rights of tenant-proprietors and others, in 1859 and again in 1884.

But in one aspect, the Settlement has not received its full meed of praise. Here, for the first time in Oriental history, was seen the spectacle of a foreign ruler binding himself and his successors to abstain from periodical revisions of the land-tax; almost creating a new race of landlords; giving to property another title than the sword of its owner or the favour of a Viceroy; and content to leave to the Zamíndárs the whole profit resulting from increased population and undisturbed peace. At this distance of time it is not very easy to estimate the exact effect of such abnegation on the minds of the great Zamíndárs of Bengal and Behar as well as on the Chiefs and Princes of neighbouring States. It is sometimes said that a policy of this kind is ascribed by natives to weakness and fear. Whatever may be the case in other instances, and however necessary it may be to rule Orientals by firmness and strict justice quite as much as by conciliation, it can hardly be said that the moderation of Cornwallis was considered as a sign of impotence. It must have been felt all over the Province as a relief, if not a blessing. And though several of the solid fruits of the Settlement in perpetuity might have been equally attained by a Settlement for a long period, it may be argued that periodical assessments might in Bengal have been productive of other evils. Bengal is, more than any other Province in India, the scene of that evasion and subterfuge which are the proverbial resources of the weak. In other Provinces, as the period for revision draws nigh, a certain amount of distrust and disquietude arises in the minds of the population. Wealth is concealed; lands are purposely thrown out of cultivation; and many unfair means are resorted to in order to avoid an increase of rental.

There can be no doubt that all these disturbing agencies would have been set actively at work in Bengal. It is not, moreover, easy to over-estimate the advantage of a wealthy and privileged class, who have everything to lose and nothing to gain by revolution.

This was clearly seen and acknowledged at the time of the Sepoy Mutiny. There were few large military cantonments in the Lower Provinces in that eventful year. The elements of a great Sepoy revolt, with its inevitable accompaniments of arson, plunder, and anarchy, were not abundant as they were in the Upper Provinces. Even when isolated detachments of Sepoys mutinied as they did at Dacca, Chittagong, and in Bírbhúm, they met with no countenance from the Zamíndárs. The Sepoys were disciplined and trained to fight. They had arms of precision in the midst of an unwarlike population, the bravest of whom could do little more than use a matchlock to kill a wild beast, and a spear to transfix an adversary in a village fight. But after the first outbreak at the Station, where they were resolutely met by a mere handful of Englishmen, the Sepoys took to the villages and the jungles, and then they literally melted away before the impassive demeanour, the want of sympathy, and the silent loyalty of the Zamíndárs. In other Provinces the system of village communities afforded no bulwark against the tide of anarchy. That system was in many respects admirable and suited to the community.

It had been justly renowned as a field for the

exhibition of the highest kind of administrative talent. Men of large experience, broad views, and active sympathies, had fashioned or had rescued from slow decay, that most wonderful and diversified piece of mosaic known as the *pattidárí* tenure. They had almost defied the teachings of political economy and had wellnigh arrested the play of social forces by rooting old and hereditary cultivators to the soil. Yet with the outbreak of the Sepoys and the temporary eclipse of British authority, these fabrics, the result of so much experience and philanthropy, collapsed of themselves or were broken up. In Bengal public tranquillity was hardly ruffled. The rebellion of Koer Sing in Behar was a solitary exception.

In times of famine and scarcity the co-operation of wealthy Zamíndárs has been invoked by the Government, and in many instances ungrudgingly afforded. Here and there, no doubt, there were cases where Zamíndárs were niggardly and selfish. But several experts hold still to the opinion that scarcity is met, relief works are set on foot, and supplies are transported with greater facility, where there are large Zamíndárís, than in Provinces where the Settlement has been made with the heads of village communities, or with each Ryot direct as in Madras. The Tirhút famine of 1873–4 is certainly an instance in point. And in a country where social distinctions and inequalities still retain their attractions for the masses, the maintenance of some large Zamíndárís is quite in accordance with native feeling, and it has political advantages which compensate or at any rate balance its defects.

But, to sum up, it can hardly now be an open question whether Shore's plea for delay would have involved any sacrifice. The Zamíndárs, with security of tenure and with privileges converted into rights, would have been willing to accept a Settlement for a long term of years. The changes in the constitution, duties, and remuneration of the Civil Service, about to be described, would have enabled the Indian Government to train up a race of officials who had a deeper knowledge of agricultural customs and a more complete mastery of administrative principles and details. At any and every periodical revision of the Zamíndárí system, abuses must have been tested by increased official knowledge, and remedies would have been applied at an earlier date. This revision would have probably outweighed any disadvantage arising out of the excitement inseparable from a break in the revenue system. As it has turned out, action for the benefit of tenants and under-tenants has been forced on the Government by the periodical representations of district officers, by the recurrence of formidable combinations on the part of the agriculturists, and by outrages for which magistrates and judges who sat in judgment on their perpetrators were often compelled to remark that there were divers excuses to be made.

Yet it must be remembered that the Settlement

of the Lower Provinces a century ago was not due to the cries of a down-trodden community and to a long discussion by well-informed writers in a free and independent press. It was what seemed to some men at the time the only way out of a series of difficulties. Taken in its purely commercial and financial aspect, it resulted in a considerable abandonment of future revenue. As an administrative measure, it obviously required much more of statutory declaration and vigorous executive management to render it complete. But looking at it solely from the political point of view, it was the means of allaying apprehensions and removing doubts, while it proved a strong incentive to good behaviour, and to something beyond passive loyalty in seditious and troublous times.

Some of the fundamental principles of the system were practical and sound. The change from the mere collecting native agent, with his status that might or might not become hereditary; the recognition, as a matter of right, of Rájás, chieftains, and other superior landlords; the grave and measured language of a Proclamation putting an end to brief and temporary contrivances for the realisation of the dues of the State; the incentives to prudent management afforded by the prospect of additional rental; and the sense of security, the limited ownership, and power of transmission and disposal, were, in theory, excellent.

Lord Cornwallis had only the experience and the legacies of failure to guide him. Pressed for ways and means, and anxious for reform in more departments than one, he committed himself to a policy which, in regard to the three interested parties—the Zamíndár, the Ryot, and the Ruling Power—assured the welfare of the first, somewhat postponed the claims of the second, and sacrificed the increment of the third.

CHAPTER IV

Reform of the Civil Service

It is almost impossible, in this attempt to describe Cornwallis as an Indian ruler, to do more than give occasional extracts from his voluminous correspondence and to state a summary of his political views. But now and then a private and confidential letter throws such a light on the perplexities which tried his constancy and statesmanship, and illustrates problems only solved after painful experience, that it is expedient to quote from it at length. Of this kind is a private and confidential letter to Dundas, dated April 4th, 1790. That minister had sent him a list of questions relating to the East India Company as a commercial and a political institution; to the right of patronage to civil appointments in India; to the export trade of the Dependency; to the relation which English forces should bear to the Sepoys; and to other matters. Changes in administration have left to some of the views of the Governor-General only their historical interest. On other points, his opinions might have weight with administrators of our own time; and his reply to Dundas is a fitting prelude to a summary of those internal and executive reforms which were to occupy so much of his time and attention, and to leave behind them such good and lasting effects.

'I must acknowledge that I am happy to hear that the principles of that plan were still under deliberation, and that it was only upon the supposition that the commercial branch might be left to the Company, and the other departments taken into the hands of Government, that you had stated these queries. Many weighty objections occur to the separation that you propose, for it is almost beyond a doubt with me that no solid advantages would be derived from placing the civil and revenue departments under the immediate direction of the King's Government; and I am perfectly convinced that if the fostering aid and protection and, what is full as important, the check and control of the governments abroad, are withdrawn from the commercial departments, the Company would not long enjoy their new charter, but must very soon be reduced to a state of actual bankruptcy.

'I am not surprised that, after the increased and vexatious contradictions which you have experienced from the Court of Directors, you should be desirous of taking as much of the business as possible entirely out of their hands; but I know that great changes are hazardous in all popular governments, and as the paltry patronage of sending out a few writers is of no value to such an administration as Mr. Pitt's, I should recommend it to your serious consideration whether it would not be wiser, when you shall no longer have to contend with chartered rights, to tie their hands from doing material mischief, without meddling with their Imperial dignity or their power of naming writers, and not to encounter the furious clamour that will be raised against annexing the patronage of India to the influence of the Crown, except in cases of the most absolute necessity.

'That a Court of Directors formed of such materials as the present can never, when left to themselves, conduct any branch of the business of this country properly, I will readily admit; but under certain restrictions and when better constituted, it might prove an useful check on the ambitious or corrupt designs of some future minister. In order, however, to enable such Directors to do this negative good, or to prevent them doing much positive evil, they should have a circumscribed management of the whole, and not a permission to ruin uncontrolled the commercial advantages which Britain should derive from her Asiatic territories.

'It will, of course, have been represented to you that the India Company formerly was supported by its commerce alone, and that it was then richer than it is at present, and that when their Directors have no longer any business with governing empires, they may again become as thrifty merchants as heretofore.

I am persuaded, however, that experience would give a contradiction to that theory, for if they should not have lost their commercial talents by having been Emperors, this country is totally changed by being under their dominion. There are now so many Europeans residing in India, and there is such a competition at every wharf of any consequence, that in my opinion even an upright Board of Trade sitting at Calcutta could not make advantageous contracts or prevent the manufactures from being debased; and therefore, that unless the Company have able and active Residents at the different factories, and unless those Residents are prevented by the power of Government from cheating them as they formerly did, London would no longer be the principal mart for the choicest commodities of India.

'If the proposed separation was to take place, not a man of credit or character would stay in the Company's service, if he could avoid it; and those who did remain, or others who might be hereafter appointed, would be soon looked upon as an inferior class of people to the servants acting under appointments from His Majesty. The contempt with which they would be treated would not pass unobserved by the natives, and would preclude the possibility of their being of essential use, even if they were not deficient in character or commercial abilities, and upon the supposition that the Company could afford to pay them liberally for their services. When you add to the evils which I have described, and which no man acquainted with this country will think fictitious, the jobbing that must prevail at the India House in a department which is in a manner given up to plunder, you will not, I am sure, think that I have gone too far in prophesying the bankruptcy of the Company.

'In answer to this statement of the impossibility of the Company's carrying on the trade when all the other parts of the administration of the country are taken into the hands of Government, it may be said by people who have reflected but little on the subject, "If the Company cannot carry on the trade, throw it open to all adventurers." To that mode I should have still greater objection, as it would be very difficult for Government to prevent this unfortunate country from being overrun by desperate speculators from all parts of the British dominions. The manufacturers would soon go to ruin, and the exports—which would annually diminish in value—would be sent indiscriminately to the different countries of Europe.

'As the new system will only take place when the rights of the present Company cease, you cannot be charged with a violation of charters, and the attacks of the Opposition in Parliament will therefore be confined to an examination of its expediency and efficacy. I fancy I need hardly repeat to you that they would above all things avail themselves of any apparent attempts on your part to give an increase of patronage to the Crown, which could not be justified on the soundest constitutional principles, or on the ground of evident necessity; and could make use of it to misrepresent your intentions and principles, and to endeavour to influence the minds of the natives against you.

'An addition of patronage to the Crown, to a certain degree, will, however, in my opinion, be not only a justifiable measure, but absolutely necessary for the future good government of this country.

'But, according to my judgment, a renewal of the Company's Charter for the management of the territorial revenues and the commerce of India for a limited time (for instance, ten or fifteen years), and under such stipulations as it may be thought proper to annex as conditions, would be the wisest foundation for your plan, both for your own sakes as Ministers, and as being best calculated for securing the greatest possible advantages to Britain from her Indian possessions, and least likely to injure the essential principles of our own Constitution.

'The present Court of Directors is so numerous, and the responsibility for public conduct which falls to the share of each individual is so small, that it can have no great weight with any of them; and the participation in a profitable contract, or the means of serving friends or providing for relations, must always more than compensate to them for the loss that they may sustain by any fluctuation that may happen in the market price of the stock which constitutes their qualifications. I should therefore think that it would be very useful to the public to reduce the number of directors to twelve or to nine; and if handsome salaries could be annexed to those situations, I should be clear for adopting means for their being prohibited from having an interest directly or indirectly in contracts, or in any commercial transactions whatever, in which the Company may have the smallest concern.

'At the same time, however, if one or both of these points should be carried, I would not by any means recommend that they should retain the power of appointing Governors, Commanders-in-Chief, or Members of Council at any of the Presidencies; the honour and interest of the nation, the fate of our fleets and armies, being too deeply staked on the conduct of the persons holding the above-mentioned offices, to render it safe to trust their nominations in any other hands but those of the Executive Government of Britain. But as this measure, though not in fact deviating very widely from the existing arrangement by which the King has the power of recalling those officers, would at first appear a strong one, and would be vehemently opposed, I would give it every qualification that the welfare and security of the country would admit of. I would establish it by law, that the choice of the civil Members of Council should be limited to Company's servants of a certain standing (at least twelve years), which would in the mind of every candid person leave very little room in respect to them for ministerial patronage, and it should be left to the Court of Directors to frame such general Regulations for the appointment to offices in India as should be consistent with the selection of capable men, and to establish the strictest system that they can devise of check and control upon every article of expenditure at the different Presidencies.

'I would likewise recommend that it should be clearly understood and declared that the Court of Directors should have a right to expect that His Majesty's Ministers should pay the greatest attention to all their representations respecting the conduct of the Governors, Commander-in-Chief, and Councillors; and that in case satisfactory redress should not be given to any of their complaints of that nature, that they should have a right to insist upon the recall of any Governor, Commander-in-Chief, or Councillors, whom they should name, and that the utmost facility should be given to them to institute prosecutions against such Governors, &c., whose conduct may appear to them to have been culpable, before the Court of Judicature which has been established by Act of Parliament for the trial of Indian delinquents.

'In regard to the military arrangements, I am clearly of opinion that the European troops should all belong to the King, for experience has shown that the Company cannot keep up an efficient European force in India; this is a fact so notorious that no military man who has been in this country will venture to deny it, and I do not care how strongly I am quoted as authority for it.

'The circumstances, however, of the native troops are very different. It is highly expedient and indeed absolutely necessary for the public good, that the officers who are destined to serve in these corps should come out at an early period of life and devote themselves entirely to the Indian service; a perfect knowledge of the language, and a minute attention to the customs and religious prejudices of the Sepoys, being qualifications for that line which cannot be dispensed with. Were these officers to make a part of the King's army, it would soon become a practice to exchange their commissions with ruined officers from England, who would be held in contempt by their inferior officers and in abhorrence by their soldiers, and you need not be told how dangerous a disaffection in our native troops would be to our existence in this country. I think, therefore, that as you cannot make laws to bind the King's prerogative in the exchange or promotions of his army, it would be much the safest determination to continue the native troops in the Company's service, and by doing so you would still leave to the Court of Directors the patronage of cadets, and of course give some popularity to the measure.

'The alternate line to be drawn would give to the Court of Directors the appointment of writers to the civil branches of the service and of cadets for the native troops, and the power of prescribing certain general rules under the description I have mentioned for the disposal of offices by the Government in India, and of calling the Governors, &c., to an immediate account for every deviation from these rules; but they ought to be strictly prohibited from appointing or recommending any of their servants to succeed to offices in this country, as such appointments or recommendàtions are more frequently granted to intrigue and solicitation, than to a due regard to real merit or good pretensions, and such interference at home must always tend in some degree to weaken the authority of the Government in India.

'Upon the supposition of the Charters being renewed, it appears to me highly requisite for the public good that the right of inspection and control in the King's Ministers should be extended to every branch of the Company's affairs, without any exception as to their commerce: and as altercations between the controlling power and the Board of Directors must always be detrimental to the public interest, whether occasioned by improper encroachments on one side or an obstinate or capricious resistance on the other, it seems particularly desirable that not only the extent, but also the manner in which the Ministers are to exercise the right of inspection and control should be prescribed so clearly as to prevent, if possible, all grounds for misapprehension or dispute.'

The establishment of a revenue system, which if not entirely new, presented one or more novel features of paramount importance, was not calculated to ensure either the prosperity of the country or the contentment of the people, unless measures were taken to reform the Civil Service and to appoint as Collectors of districts men who could be relied on as proof against corruption. When Cornwallis landed in India, the whole service was more or less in a transition state. It was still occupied with commercial enterprise, and yet its members were called on to discharge administrative functions and to fill executive posts. They were often remunerated by gratuities and commission, and the acceptance by them of large gratuities and of perquisites was common. It was the survival of an even worse state of things when men in the high position of Members of Council had not scrupled to accept lacks of rupees for giving a preference to one Nawáb or pretender over another. There had been flagrant instances of corruption at Lucknow, Benares, and Madras, and it must be admitted that the Court of Directors had seen and almost approved a system under which their servants, placed in positions of high trust and of manifold temptations, drew small salaries and were allowed to make up for this deficiency by large extra lump sums. Even when the Governor-General represented in strong language the necessity for some reform, the Directors were still of opinion that Collectors should be paid partly by commission and partly by fixed salaries, but that the larger part of their remuneration should be the commission.

The Resident at Benares, who really wielded almost absolute power in that Province without check or control, drew only 1000 rupees a month, but from monopolies in commercial and other ventures, received besides four lacks every year. In other places, Collectors engaged in commercial speculation under cover of the name of some relative or friend, and it may be said roundly, that while no Collector drew above 1200 rupees a month, his irregular and additional gains amounted to far more. Cornwallis saw almost at once that the only mode of preventing abuses, maintaining discipline, and creating a sense of honour and responsibility, was to give liberal salaries and to confine the recipients to their proper work. Trading was henceforth forbidden; and if commission was still allowed, it was calculated at so much per cent. on the net collections. Even this regulated mode of payment, though perfectly fair and equitable at the time of its introduction, was eventually abolished.

There were other anomalies in the constitution and character of the service which could not escape notice. The criminal administration had been left in the hands of the Nawáb Názim and his native subordinates, as will be explained in dealing with the new arrangements for civil and criminal justice. The

Collectors from the time of Warren Hastings, besides being responsible for the revenue, were vested with certain judicial powers in civil cases. Cornwallis goes so far as to state that the Civil Courts of justice throughout the whole of the Company's Provinces had been for many years in the hands of the Company's servants. The Collector, in addition to his revenue duties, held in this capacity what was termed a Mál Adálat, or court in which he decided all cases regarding the rights of the landholders and cultivators, and all claims arising between them and their servants. It was resolved to abolish these Mál Adálats, in which the civil servant was Judge as well as Collector, and to transfer all judicial powers and the decision of all rights and all civil suits to regular judicial tribunals. It may here be mentioned by anticipation that six years after the departure of Cornwallis, Collectors were again vested with power to settle, in a summary enquiry, all claims for the rent of the current year due from ryots to Zamíndárs.

But with this exception the Collector, after 1793, was confined to his proper functions, which were quite sufficient to occupy his attention and to increase his store of official knowledge. The districts over which such Collectors presided were enormous in extent. The district of Jessor touched the Twenty-four Parganás on one side and the Rájsháhí District across the Ganges on the other; and it was not for thirty or forty years afterwards that the size of these and other zillahs were curtailed by the formation of smaller independent districts, such as Bárásat, Bográ, Pabná, and others.

The Collector, to sum up, was placed by Cornwallis in a definite, important, well-salaried post. He was responsible for the land revenue of a vast tract, which in amount varied from ten to twenty lacks of rupees. He looked after the estates of minors, and of landowners incapacitated by lunacy or other causes. He was the Superintendent of all estates held *khás*, as it is termed, on those in which the Government had acquired the Zamíndárí or landholder's, as well as the sovereign right. He was paymaster of pensioners and allowances for compensation. He was the recognised authority for the division of estates between irreconcilable shareholders. He alone could apportion the liability for revenue of each share. He collected the tax on spirituous liquors. He was to put up the estates of defaulting proprietors to public sale. He was formally placed under the Board of Revenue, with which he was regularly to correspond.

The popular idea of a Collector in England is or was an individual with a note-book and certain forms and schedules and demands, calling at inconvenient times for the Queen's taxes or the parish rates, and viewed with aversion and dislike by householders. From the time of Cornwallis the Anglo-Indian collector became a Court of Wards, as well as a Court of Exchequer, and on his moderation, good faith, skill, and management, there depended the welfare of inhabitants who even in those epochs of forest waste and jungle, not seldom amounted to a half or one million of souls in a single district: together with the realisation of the State dues.

The Perpetual Settlement and the relegation of the Collectors to their proper and essential duties was now accomplished. But a great deal remained to be done before the Civil Service could be said to have entered on the entire executive and judicial administration of Bengal and Behar. The machinery for the detection and punishment of crime had been left, as already remarked, in the hands of the Nawáb Názim, who might be termed the titular sovereign of the country. The consequences were ruinous to property and life. The Faujdár of Húglí, a metropolitan district, received ten thousand pounds or a lack of rupees a year, and *dakáiti*, or gang robbery with violence, was rife in the very neighbourhood of Calcutta, on the confines of the Maráthá Ditch, and indeed all over the Lower Provinces.

Criminal trials were conducted by native Judges. It is true that there was already a Court of Appeal known as the Sadr Diwání and Nizámat Adálat, and that the English Collector of revenue was supposed to overlook the proceedings of the native magistrates in the districts; to see that witnesses were duly examined; and that the proceedings were conducted with some fairness and impartiality. But the preamble to several of the Regulations or Laws of 1793, shows that there must have been much confusion, diversity of practice, and uncertainty of jurisdiction in the civil and criminal courts. Indeed, the language of the preamble of one of these laws is so significant and illustrative of the incompetence of the native officers, and of the inability of the English Collector to interfere to any good purpose, that it must be here quoted *in extenso.* In Reg. IX of 1793 the Governor-General sums up the case for a complete change in the following terms:—

'I. Pursuant to the Regulations passed by the President and Council on 21st August, 1772, Criminal Courts, denominated Faujdárí Adálats, were established in the interior parts of the Provinces for the trial of persons charged with crimes or misdemeanors: and the Collectors of the revenue, who were covenanted servants of the Company, were directed to superintend the proceedings of the officers of those Courts, and on trials to see that the necessary witnesses were summoned and examined, that due weight was allowed to their testimony, and that the decisions passed were fair and impartial. By the same Regulations, a separate and superior Criminal Court was established at Murshidábád, under the denomination of the Nizámat Adálat, for revising the proceedings of the Provincial Criminal Courts in capital cases, and the Committee of Revenue at Murshidábád was vested with a control over this court, similar to that which the Collectors of the revenue were empowered to exercise over the Provincial Courts. Upon the abolition of the Committee of Revenue at Murshidábád, the Nizámat Adálat was removed to Calcutta, and placed under the charge of a Dárogha or superintendent, subject to the control of the President of the Council, who revised the sentences of the Criminal Courts in capital cases. The above arrangements continued in force, without any considerable alteration, until 18th October, 1775, when the entire control over the department of criminal justice was committed to the Náib Názim. The Nizámat Adálat was in consequence re-established at Murshidábád, and the Náib Názim appointed native officers, denominated Faujdárs, assisted by persons versed in the Muhammadan law, to superintend the Criminal Courts in the several districts, and to apprehend and bring to trial offenders against the public peace. This system was adhered to, without any material variation, until 6th April, 1781, when the institution of Faujdárs not having answered the intended purposes, the general establishment both of Faujdárs, and the Thánádárs or police officers acting under them, were abolished. Faujdárí Courts, however, were continued in the several divisions, subject as before to the control of the Náib Názim or superintendent of the Nizámat Adálat, and the English judges of the Courts of Diwání Adálat were appointed magistrates, with a power to apprehend *dakáitis* and persons charged with crimes or misdemeanors within their respective jurisdictions and commit them to the nearest Faujdárí Court for trial. With a view to enable Government to superintend, in some degree, the administration of justice in criminal cases, a separate department was at the same time established at the Presidency, under the control of the Governor-General, to receive monthly returns of the sentences passed in the Faujdárí Courts: and for the assistance of the Governor-General in this duty, a Covenanted Civil servant of the Company was appointed with the official appellation of Remembrancer to the Criminal Courts.

'From the inefficiency, however, of the authority of the

English magistrates over the Zamíndárs and other land-holders, the administration of justice in criminal cases was much impeded, whilst the Regulation which vested the magistrates with the power of apprehending offenders, but without permitting them to interfere in any respect in the trials, gave rise to a new evil. The magistrates being obliged to deliver over to the Dároghas, or superintendents of the Faujdárí Courts, all persons charged with a breach of the peace, however trivial, and a considerable time often elapsing before they were brought to trial, many of the lowest and most indigent classes of the people were frequently detained for a long period in prison, where their sufferings often exceeded the degree of their criminality. The magistrates therefore on 27th June, 1787, were vested with authority to hear and decide on complaints of petty affrays, abusive names, and other slight offences, and under certain restrictions to inflict corporal punishment and impose fines on the offenders.

'But the numerous robberies, murders, and other enormities, which continued to be daily committed throughout the country, evincing that the administration of criminal justice was still in a very defective state; and as these evils appeared to result principally from the great delay which occurred in bringing offenders to punishment, and to the law not being duly enforced, as well as to other material defects in the Constitution of the Criminal Courts; and as it was essential for the prevention of crimes not only that offenders should be deprived of the means of eluding the pursuit of the officers of justice, but that they should be speedily and impartially tried when apprehended; the Governor-General in Council passed certain Regulations on 3rd December, 1790, establishing Courts of Circuit under the superintendence of English Judges assisted by natives versed in the Muhammadan law, for trying in the first instance persons charged with crimes or misdemeanors, and enabling the Governor-General and the members of the Supreme Council to sit in the Nizámat Adálat (which were for that purpose again removed to Calcutta) and superintend the administration of criminal justice throughout the provinces. These Regulations, with the subsequent amendments, are now re-enacted with further alterations and modifications[1].'

The above quotation from the new Code of this time, with other like deliverances, is illustrative of the extreme caution with which the Government proceeded to assume its responsibilities and to carry out reforms. These changes to readers and administrators of the present generation seem easy and natural. Collectors who could only advise native Judges—English magistrates who might apprehend and yet not try criminals—a Government which

[1] The author of this memoir in his early years of service discovered some of the old records of those very Criminal Courts, presided over by these Faujdárs, still in existence, and on inspecting them he found what is known as the Rúbakárí, or finding and sentence of the Court. It was very brief and concise, and ended with the direction that the prisoner *kaid bashad*: in other words, that he was to be sent to prison. No term whatever was specified, and there was a tradition amongst the older native employés of the magistrates' office as late as the year 1845, of an individual who, having been sentenced to indefinite imprisonment for stealing some of a neighbour's rice crop, remained in durance for many years. It must be added that the rules of prison discipline were neither then, nor for many years afterwards, of a strict nature. Prisoners were locked up at night, but during the day they had a good deal of liberty, walked about the bázárs, did or pretended to do a little work in repairing the roads and clearing out the ditches of this Station, saw their friends, and often obtained tobacco, sweetmeats, and other indulgences.

acted as a sort of referee, which might prevent unjust sentences in capital cases, but could not interfere to any valid purpose in the earlier stages of an assize, were evidently not the agencies fitted to deal with a population which, however unwarlike and generally tractable, contained in towns and villages many of the elements of crime and disorder. Cornwallis, after some tentative measures, proceeded to map out the whole of the country into districts presided over by English Judges and Magistrates. In some twenty-five of these districts or zillahs he appointed a Civil and Sessions Judge. In four of the principal cities—that is, in Calcutta, Patná, Dacca, and Murshidábád—he established Provincial Courts of Appeal, or courts intermediate between the Court of the Zillah and the Sadr Court, or highest and ultimate tribunal. Another law extended and defined the jurisdiction of the last-mentioned court. Distinct and, in some instances, minute rules of procedure were incorporated in these laws.

Magistrates with judicial powers of reasonable extent were appointed to each district, and Darogahs or heads of police were placed under them for the prevention and detection of crime. In civil suits the English Judge was empowered to hear and decide all suits regarding real and personal property, land rents, debts, accounts, partnerships, marriage, caste, inheritance, damages, and, in short, all cases of a civil nature. In criminal trials the Code to be followed was the Muhammadan Code; but means were at once taken to mitigate its harshness and to correct its absurdities. Barbarous punishments, such as mutilation, were not allowed. The rules of Muhammadan evidence were modified and brought into harmony with those of English courts. In civil cases between Hindus the Judge was assisted by a native Pandit, who advised on matters of inheritance, marriage, caste, and the like. The Muhammadan law similarly was applied in cases where both parties were Musalmáns. When the litigants were of different creeds, the English Judge was to follow the dictates of equity and good conscience. Of his native coadjutors, the Pandit was the first to be abolished, though he lasted till 1821. But the office of Kází or Maulaví remained in some districts down to the introduction of the Penal Code and the Code of Criminal Procedure in 1860.

While attempts had been made by Warren Hastings and by Cornwallis himself to improve the civil and criminal administration of the province, and though a few changes and improvements had been introduced all tending to vest authority more and more in the hands of Englishmen, the system in its fulness dates from 1793, the last year of the Cornwallis administration. Every civil servant from the beginning of this century has looked on this date as the commencement of a new era. He may have heard of other 'General Regulations,' but they were never printed or circulated for his use and guidance.

The Cornwallis Code, whether for revenue, police criminal and civil justice, or other functions, defined and set bounds to authority, created procedure, by a regular system of appeal guarded against the miscarriage of justice, and founded the Civil Service of India as it exists to this day. This Code has been the basis of every attempt to introduce law and order into each successive acquisition of districts and kingdoms. Very possibly its provisions were in some instances cumbrous and minute, and not suited to races more manly and warlike and less prone to litigation and chicanery than the population of Central and Lower Bengal. Some of its sections and clauses were ruthlessly put aside when new, simple, and equitable Codes had to be suited to purely savage or warlike tribes. It may be also said that criminals were allowed a fatal facility of appeal, which in the working proved disadvantageous to the general welfare of the community. But the Cornwallis Code was dictated by an anxious desire to conciliate Hindus and Muhammadans, to soothe their feelings, to avoid offence to religious and social prejudices, and at the same time to substitute order, method, and system for anarchy, chaos, and the irregular and uncontrolled exercise of judicial power. Objections have occasionally been made to the phraseology of these Regulations, and doubtless they suffer by comparison with the precise, correct, and luminous language of the later Acts dating from 1833, when the legislation of the Indian Government was framed by such high authorities as Macaulay and Cameron, or Maine and Stephen in our own days. But we should remember that the Indian Government a century ago had to deal with a community ruled by despots and unacquainted with any fixed or settled Code of administration. The training of the officials who were to administer the new laws was imperfect. Many of the Collectors and Magistrates began to learn their business when they began to work, and had to arrive at system and method through the detection of errors and mistakes.

The Regulations in consequence were not merely the expression of what in future was to be the revenue or the criminal law of the land. The preambles, and occasionally some of the sections, contained reasons and explanations for the new procedure. Some are more in the nature of a manifesto from the Ruling Power than a law. The Governor-General reviewed the past, pointed out the errors discovered in practice and arising out of imperfect knowledge of the wants of the people, and then proceeded to apply a legislative remedy.

The Perpetual Settlement itself took the form of a Proclamation which became Regulation I in the Code. The Hindus, 'who form the body of the people,' are expressly informed that while agriculture then as now is the principal element in the wealth of the country, it is the object of the British Government to extend commerce, to improve judicial procedure, and to provide against the recurrence of inundation and drought.

In addition to his revenue and judicial Code, Lord Cornwallis laid it down as a rule that the official acts of the Collectors might be challenged in the Civil Courts of the country; that Government might be sued, like any private individual, for exactions or infringements of the rights of landholders; and that such suits could only be cognizable by Judges who had no direct or personal interest in enforcing the financial claims of Government. Practically the Governor-General did away with any idea that a Collector was a sort of pro-consul whose irregularities were exempt from the jurisdiction of the ordinary tribunals, and who was accountable only to the Executive which he served. Many important subjects, political and military, were of course exempted from the cognizance of the law courts. But from 1793, in all that related to landed and personal property, the Government, in the language of one of the Regulations, 'divested itself of the power of infringing in its executive capacity on the rights and privileges' which, in its legislative capacity, it had conferred on the landholders.

Divers other important questions continued to occupy the attention of Cornwallis. There was considerable jealousy between the English officers of the King's troops or Royals, as they were termed, and the officers of native infantry. The sovereign of England was not likely ever to give up the notion that officers bearing his commission were entitled to a pre-eminence over those who held their appointments from a commercial body of his own subjects. It was calculated that at that epoch the whole European and native forces of Bengal and Madras did not exceed 70,000 men. Of these, 5000 only were King's troops; the Company's 'Europeans,' or Englishmen recruited by the Company in England, were about the same in number.

These latter were 'a set of wretched objects;' and Cornwallis saw at once that in order to raise them to the standard, the discipline, and the efficiency to which they subsequently attained, the Directors should be allowed to recruit openly, and the recruits should be subjected to martial law, and be placed under the command of their own officers until the date of their embarkation for the East. Dundas looked far ahead, and actually prepared a memorandum for the amalgamation of the Royal and the Company's troops into one army. Cornwallis admitted that if the Company's troops consisted only of Englishmen the amalgamation would be a very easy matter. But he saw a great difficulty in dealing with nearly four hundred officers serving in native regiments, who were, as a rule, the best men in the army, and who were well acquainted with the languages, manners, and religious customs of the Sepoys. So the amalgamation was deferred for three quarters of a century, but a scheme originating with Cornwallis was eventually carried out, by which the Company's officers were allowed to take rank equally with those of the Royal regiments, according to the dates of their respective commissions, while serving in India. Jealousy between the two sets of officers—though always kept within bounds in action and in a campaign, owing to a sense of military subordination—occasionally came to the surface in peaceful times; but it would not be easy to find any instances in which military operations were impeded or marred by any such social antipathy. Some of the most signal victories in India have been gained by Company's officers commanding a combined force of the soldiers of the Sovereign and the Sepoys of the Company. With all his philanthropy and considerate regard for the feelings of the natives, Cornwallis was quite alive to one danger to which India has never at any time been unexposed.

'It must be universally admitted,' he tells the Court of Directors, 'that without a large and well-regulated body of Europeans, our hold of these valuable dominions must be very insecure. It cannot be expected that even the best of treatment would constantly conciliate the willing obedience of so vast a body of people, differing from ourselves in almost every circumstance of laws, religion, and customs; and oppression of individuals, errors of government, and several other unforeseen causes, will no doubt arouse an inclination to revolt. On such occasions it would not be wise to place great dependence upon their countrymen who compose the native regiments to secure their subjection.' It was not the Governor-General's last utterance, but it might be said, 'Illa tanquam cycnea fuit . . . hominis vox et oratio.'

CHAPTER V

PRIVATE LIFE AND SOCIAL CUSTOMS

WHILE Cornwallis's relations with Henry Dundas were, even when they differed, of the most amicable nature, and while their correspondence is replete with instructive and statesmanlike views on most of the vital portions of Indian administration, it is clear that his endeavours to promote the efficiency of the Civil Service were sorely hampered by requests from sundry high personages in England to promote their relatives and friends. The Civil Service was not then regularly fenced in by exclusive rules and rigid restrictions, and there were divers occasions on which the Head of the Government might exercise his discretion in giving appointments to candidates who had not been sent out by the Court, or who had gone out on their own account, as the saying was. In the hands of a strong and just man it was not likely that the privilege of selection outside the ranks of the service would be abused. But peers and other acquaintances had not the slightest hesitation in writing out to Cornwallis to provide for Mr. Such-a-one in some lucrative and easy post. To one peer he had to reply that he had never heard of a certain clerical friend, but unless he had been sent out by the Court of Directors it was not in his power to promote him.

In the same letter he says he should be glad to appoint a Mr. Beachcroft to a Commercial Residency if he were likely to succeed in it: 'But here, my lord, we are in the habit of looking for the man for the place, and not for the place for the man.' Another peer recommends a young gentleman named Ramus, a late page of honour to the King. He went out as a free merchant. The name of Ramus occurs about this time in the list of Company's servants. But the most flagrant attempt in this direction was made by the Prince of Wales. He had a *protégé* named Treves, whose ambition it was to be appointed to the Adálat, or Civil Court of Benares. The post at that time was filled by 'a black named Ali Cann.' This gentleman's right name was Alí Ibráhím Khán, a man of real talent and universally respected. Cornwallis answers His Royal Highness to the effect that though he was anxious to put the Company's servants at the head of both the Civil and Criminal Courts, it would be a difficult and unpopular measure to remove the incumbent, and that if Alí Khán were to die to-morrow, it would be impossible to give this appointment to Mr. Treves, looking to his standing in the service, as well as the impropriety of appointing so young a man to a situation of so much gravity and importance.

Again, a year afterwards, the Prince of Wales

recommends a young Mr. Watts, who wanted to get a rank in the 'regulars' equal to what he had in the Company's army. But he was told civilly that this could not be done, and Mr. Watts afterwards obtained a commission in a West India regiment. These recommendations, in a letter to his brother the Bishop of Lichfield, are treated by the Governor-General as 'infamous and unjustifiable jobs.'

Other difficulties had to be met and overcome. On one occasion the Prince recommends a young man going out as a cadet, but in a harmless way and for such social notice as the Governor-General may think fit. On another point the Court of Directors very properly came to his aid. The Court had strong objections to recognise as agents persons accredited in England by such potentates as the Nawáb of Bengal and the Rájá of Tanjore. The Directors held that all communications from Princes or Chiefs deeming themselves aggrieved, should be preferred only through the regular channel of the Indian Government. And this sound precedent has rarely been set aside, and never without risk and prejudice to good administration. Acting in the same spirit, Cornwallis absolutely refused to forward a complimentary letter from the Nawáb Vizier of Oudh, accompanied by 25,000 rupees, for Dr. Willis, the King's physician.

A *nazr* of 101 gold mohurs, as a congratulatory offering from an inferior to a superior, with a sum of 7000 rupees for Dr. Willis, and an additional 7000 rupees for the poor in the neighbourhood of the King's palace, transmitted by the Nawáb of Bengal, were all courteously but firmly refused. The Governor-General contented himself with sending the letters which accompanied these presents, to His Majesty the King of England.

Cornwallis's annoyance at the importunities of friends on behalf of candidates for office, breaks out amusingly in the letter to Lord Sydney already quoted: 'I think I told you how much Lord Ailesbury had distressed me by sending out Mr. Ritso. He is now writing in the secretary's office for 200 or 250 rupees per month, and I do not see the probability of my being able to give him anything better, without deserving to be impeached. I am still persecuted every day by people coming out with letters to me, who either get into jail or starve in the foreign Settlements. For God's sake do all in your power to stop this madness.' The Mr. Ritso alluded to was evidently employed in the secretariat as a copyist, or what used to be denominated a section-writer. Men of this class in later days were generally Eurasians, and they were remunerated by payment for so many words. Originally the rate was 750 words the rupee, but secretaries of an economical turn raised the rate of work to 1400 words.

It is pleasant after this denunciation of jobbery to turn to letters from Warren Hastings to the Governor-General. There are several allusions, in the Ross edition of the Correspondence, to the impeachment of the ex-Governor-General; and the editor expressly states that Cornwallis entertained a very high opinion of his eminent and ill-treated predecessor. The public journals of the time show that the enlightened opinion of the Settlement, as it was termed, was entirely on the side of Hastings; and at the news of his acquittal, the city of Calcutta was illuminated, and messages of congratulation were forwarded by a large number of inhabitants convened at a public meeting by the sheriff. Macaulay was well informed when he wrote that every ship that sailed from Calcutta brought home a 'cuddy-full' of friends and admirers of Hastings. But Cornwallis would take no active part in getting up testimonials to character, and the letter referring to this determination is so honourable to both Statesmen, that it is worth quoting. On the 22nd of April, 1790, Hastings writes:—

'Of thanks I have a large debt due from me to your Lordship for many and substantial favours: for your great goodness to my old domesticks; for your distinguished notice of my friends; and for the liberal manner in which you were pleased to proclaim your allowance of the testimonials which were subscribed in my favour, and to authenticate them by the transmission of them to the Court of Directors. . . . You might, my Lord, have done more to indicate your countenance of those subscriptions, had I been entitled to such a proof of your personal good-will;

but though I should have felt as I ought for the motive, I should have regretted that you had yielded to it. Such a proceeding would have been construed into a transgression of the line of public duty, and have defeated its own purpose, by inducing a suspicion that the testimonials were extorted by the influence of authority. Considering the subject in its relation to your Lordship, I applaud the nice discretion with which you tempered a conduct impelled by a desire to promote the redress of an injured character. Regarding it merely as it affected myself, I am thankful for what you did, and for stopping precisely where you did stop.'

In January of the same year (1788) Cornwallis had written to Lord Sydney: 'Without entering into the merits of the case, I am very sorry that things have gone so much against poor Hastings, for he certainly has many amiable qualities;' and the writer follows this up by some uncomplimentary remarks about Impey. This may be a surprise to readers drawing their notions of Hastings from Macaulay, who thought 'his heart was somewhat hard.' The real truth is that Hastings, confronted with some spiteful adversaries, was a man of strong affections, and had a circle of many devoted and high-minded friends. His character and conduct have been recently placed in a very different light by Sir Fitzjames Stephen and Sir Alfred Lyall, and the time is possibly coming when men of the present generation may regret to think that their forefathers were his mistaken and relentless foes.

The private life of Cornwallis in his high office was pure and consistent, and marked by a wish to avoid display whenever this could be done without a disregard of the hospitality and ceremony looked for at Government House. The editor of the Correspondence notes that Cornwallis rose early, as some officials still do in India, all the year round; mounted a hard-trotting horse; and took a long ride attended by his military secretary and a groom. At table he was abstemious and even sparing in his diet. The soundest medical authorities hold that health in India is best preserved by a generous diet not carried to excess. It has been said by Sir John Kaye that there is scarcely room for personal luxury in India. What, indeed, are superfluities in temperate climates are the absolute necessaries for Indian existence and comfort. The youngest civilian or subaltern writes, eats, and usually sleeps under a punkah for more than half the year, and changes his linen twice in the day, equally with the Viceroy and the Commander-in-Chief. Routine and regularity are, in fact, prescribed by the inexorable laws of nature for the greater part of the year.

As a general rule it may be laid down, that most men in India go to bed about 10.30 or 11 and rise earlier than they do in England; and that very much of the best work in India, in the shape of Minutes, judgments, reports, correspondence with superiors and subordinates, and visits to jails and police-stations, is accomplished before breakfast.

Cornwallis writes to his son, Lord Brome, an Etonian, that life at Calcutta was perfect 'clockwork.' 'I get on horseback just as the dawn of day begins to appear, ride on the same road and the same distance, pass the whole forenoon after my return from riding in doing business, and almost exactly the same portion of time every day at table, drive out in a phaeton a little before sunset, then write or read over letters or papers on business for two hours; sit down at nine with two or three officers of my family to some fruit and a biscuit, and go to bed soon after the clock strikes ten. I don't think the greatest sap at Eton can lead a duller life than this.' In explanation of the above it should be remembered that the usual dinner-hour at Calcutta in those days was 4 p.m., and the evening meal alluded to in the above letter was a kind of light supper. Hours have long altered much for the better, and nearly everybody in India dines at 8 p.m., or at 7.30 at earliest, after the evening ride or drive.

By many persons the early morning ride has now been given up, at least during the hot weather and rains. In the glorious cold season, the race-course and the cantonment, the Mall and the parade, are full of life and animation. In those times no hill-stations had been acquired or discovered. There were no steamers to convey invalids or hard-worked officials to Madras, Rangoon, Singapur, or Galle, for a week or fortnight's sea air. The splendid Government House which overlooks the Esplanade of Calcutta, was a later creation of Lord Wellesley, and there was no suburban retreat, like the country house at Barrackpur, to which the Viceroy could retire after the weekly council on Friday to the following Monday or Tuesday. Cornwallis, however, made the best of his dull life, as Warren Hastings had done before him, and many Judges, Councillors, secretaries and staff-officers have done since. Sir William Jones, the great Orientalist and Judge, who was consulted by the Governor-General on proposed changes in the criminal law, lived at Garden Reach, three or four miles out of Calcutta, and he also had his country house at Krishnagar, the head Station of the district Nadiyá, sixty miles off, easily reached by boat or palanquin. The ruins of this house were plainly visible forty years ago in the grounds now occupied by the Krishnagar College. Cornwallis, though he did not anticipate the ceremonial and show of Lord Wellesley who attended public worship on Sunday in his robes of state, and who issued an order prohibiting all servants of Government from horse-racing on Sunday, set an excellent example of public morality.

Nor was he niggardly in public entertainments. He writes, in 1792, to his brother the Bishop, that he had been considerably out of pocket by the war with Tipú. 'I spent £27,360, reckoning the current rupee at two shillings, between the 1st of December, 1790, and the 31st of July, 1792, besides the wine from England, and two Arabian horses for which I am to give English hunters.' The general simplicity of Cornwallis's habits was a well-remembered tradition in Calcutta society, and is happily hit off in some excellent stanzas by the late H. M. Parker, Bengal C. S.[1], in his Elegy on Mr. Simms, an imaginary Tim Linkinwater, clerk in one of the great mercantile houses, as follows:—

'And he was full of anecdote, and spiced his prime pale ale
With many a curious bit of talk and many a curious tale:—
How Dexter[2] ate his buttons off; and in a one-horse-chay
My Lord Cornwallis drove about; Alack and well-a-day.'

This tradition obviously alludes to the unostentatious habits of the man. As the head of society he gave sumptuous entertainments on public festivals and holidays, as the subjoined extracts from the newspapers of the day attest[3]:—

'A very large and respectable company, in consequence of the invitation given by the Right Honourable the Governor-General, assembled on New Year's Day at the old Court House Street, where an elegant

[1] *Bole Pongis*, 2 vols. By Henry Meredith Parker. Elegy on Mr. Simms.

[2] Dexter was a livery-stable keeper at the end of the last century.

[3] Selections from *Calcutta Gazette*. By the Author.

dinner was prepared. The toasts were, as usual, echoed from the cannon's mouth, and merited this distinction from their loyalty and patriotism. In the evening the ball exhibited a circle less extensive, but equally brilliant and beautiful, with that which graced the entertainment in honour of the King's birthday. Lady Chambers and Col. Pearse danced the first minuet, and the succeeding ones continued till about half after eleven o'clock, when the supper tables presented every requisite to gratify the most refined epicurean.'

The King's birthday was the 4th of June, but was kept in Calcutta in the cold season. Colonel Pearse was a distinguished officer of artillery, and Lady Chambers was the wife of Sir Robert Chambers, one of the Puisne Judges of the Supreme Court.

Cornwallis does not appear to have found the time or to have acknowledged the necessity for many visits to the interior. Lord Wellesley spent months in a tedious journey to the North-West Provinces, by boat, stopping at all the principal stations on the Ganges. But Cornwallis for two seasons was much occupied in the Madras Presidency with the campaign against Tipú. And during the earlier years of his administration, the work that he had to do was precisely of that kind which could best be accomplished by conference with his colleagues, and by an exchange of notes and Minutes. Until he had reformed and re-constituted the Civil Service, and had laid down the principles which were to guide the Government in assessing and collecting the revenue, there was really no department to overhaul or inspect. Personal inspection of the records at Murshidábád, Patná, and Dacca, would have given him nothing that he could not equally well obtain at the Presidency; and except once, there was no necessity for those visits to the frontier and to large centres of civilisation, which have become a part of the regular duty of Viceroys and Governors, and by which the whole machinery of administration is examined, tested, and improved.

It has been shown that the Governor-General, besides being President of the Board of Revenue, was also *ex officio* a member of the Sadr Court, or Highest Civil and Criminal Court of Appeal. In one of the old reports of the decisions of that tribunal, it is expressly mentioned that the Governor-General was present as a member of the Court. But in all probability he took no active part in any discussion or argument, and merely went on a solitary occasion as a matter of form. More remarkable is it that in his letters there is no mention of the practice of duelling, which from contemporary records and newspapers was then very prevalent in India. Perhaps to a military officer such events appeared matters of course, required by the prevailing code of honour. But he thought much of the condition and treatment of the natives, and when the officers of a court-martial acquitted one of their comrades charged with the brutal treatment of a poor native, in the teeth of the clearest evidence, the Governor-General rebuked the offenders in a scathing Minute which might have come from the pen of Dalhousie or Canning.

Allusions to sport occur occasionally. The partridge shooting at Culford was good, especially in November and December. And as the practice of driving birds was then unknown, it may be presumed that there was more cover in the fields than we see anywhere at present. But we do not find any mention of a tiger, a deer, or a buffalo hunt in any of the most familiar correspondence, though districts now entirely cleared of tree and grass jungle, numbering countless villages and containing a population of 500 souls to the square mile, were then the haunts of deer, wild boars, leopards, and tigers.

Some further details of the social condition of Calcutta are subjoined. They illustrate the habits and fashions of our grandfathers in India, and shed a pleasant light on the character and position of the Governor-General.

Cornwallis was not so taken up with big questions that he could find no time for measures affecting the health and comfort of the residents of Calcutta. Within a year of his arrival he, as Governor of Fort William—an office held with but independent of that of the Governor-Generalship—forbade inmates of the Fort to use flaring links and torches, but allowed the use of lanterns with candles along the ramparts and in the streets. He tells gangs of Coffres, Manilla men and Malays, that as they had been guilty of great irregularities, and had committed outrages in Calcutta and its environs, they should ship themselves off, before a certain date, lest a worse thing befall them.

He finds time to witness the artillery practice with mortars and shells at Dum Dum, under the direction of Colonel Pearse. He attends the consecration of the new church, which is now known as the old Cathedral to distinguish it from the edifice built in the episcopate of Bishop Wilson. In the year 1787 he visited Benares, going up the Ganges in the State barge, and it was justly considered a marvellous rate of progress when an editor could record that including stoppages at divers stations on the river, Krishnagar, Bhágalpur, Patná, and others, he arrived at Benares in a month. One result of this visit was that he prohibited not only Europeans generally, but persons in the civil and military services, from proceeding beyond Baksár without an official pass. The tour also brought to his notice the melancholy fact that many of the subalterns in the army had got deeply into debt, owing to dissipation and extravagance. This state of things had been made the subject of complaint by a respectable English merchant stationed at Cawnpur, who had lent divers sums to officers and had no means of recovering his debts except by a tedious journey to Calcutta and an action in the Supreme Court.

It was not indeed till the time of Lord Auckland that all Englishmen in the interior were made amenable to the ordinary Civil Courts of the country. What Cornwallis could then do was to warn the indebted officers that he might take steps to bring them within or near the jurisdiction of the only Court that could take cognizance of such claims. At the same time officers of the army in general were further warned against opposing sheriffs' officers in the execution of their duty 'at any of the Stations, but even in the most remote districts of the Province.' It may, however, be doubted whether such functionaries were likely to be found serving processes and executing warrants in Upper India or anywhere except in the immediate neighbourhood of Calcutta. Then we have notices of more dinners, balls, suppers, and entertainments, and an instructive commentary on the inefficiency of the police while in native hands, in the occurrence of a *dakáití* in the very heart of Calcutta, when the robbers carried off some 4000 rupees.

A Proclamation against slavery by the Governor-General in Council shows that the practice of kidnapping children and sending them into the interior, or carrying them off to foreign parts, must have been not uncommon. Another order prohibited the sale and transport of guns, cannon, and warlike stores to any part of India without a pass. A third establishes a Government Stud in the district of Tirhút, and invites owners of mares to send their animals to the superintendent. This establishment existed down to very recent times. The financial difficulties under which Cornwallis and his successors laboured are illustrated by notifications that promissory notes issued for three or four months bore interest at twelve per cent.; and in no case does it seem that Government could raise money at a less interest than six per cent. Eight and ten per cent. were not uncommon. At one period during the campaign of 1791 against Tipú, the Court of Directors thought it necessary to send out specie to Madras to the amount of half a million.

It is somewhat remarkable that there is no record of any public demonstration at the time when Cornwallis gave up his high office. On August 15, 1793, he left Government House, spent the day with his successor, Sir John Shore, at Garden Reach, and embarked on a Pilot schooner, which was to take him to his ship lying off Kedgeree. But the campaign ending with Seringapatam and his return from Madras had previously been the occasion of great festivities. Englishmen and natives presented him with loyal addresses. Odes were published in the newspapers. The officers stationed at Fort William invited him to a splendid ball and supper at the theatre, which was appropriately decorated, so says the chronicler of this event, with busts of Augustus and Trajan, together with the restoration of the Roman eagle and standards to the former, and the submission of the Dacian chiefs to the latter Emperor. A year after Cornwallis's retirement his health was still drunk at the annual dinner given on St. Andrew's day, with all the warmth usually displayed by Scotchmen on such festive occasions.

There can be no doubt that in an administration of six years Cornwallis had never forfeited the regard and esteem of the English community, while he had secured a place in the memory of the natives by devoting a large portion of his time to their best interests. His position as Chief of the army as well as Governor-General at the head of the Civil Service, and the *novitas regni*, offered him advantages which in the case of a modern Viceroy it would be vain to expect. This portion of the memoir may fittingly be concluded with his reply to an address from the British inhabitants of Calcutta, forwarded to him through the Court of Directors, a year and a half after he had left India.

Writing on the 16th of April, 1795, to the chairman of the Calcutta meeting, he says:—

'I beg leave to trouble you to inform the gentlemen who signed the address that I feel myself no less flattered and honoured by the favourable opinion which so respectable a body of people have been pleased to deduce of my public and private conduct in the government of Bengal, than by the kind and cordial terms in which that opinion has been expressed.

'I likewise request that you and all the other subscribers will believe that I shall ever remember through life how much I was indebted to the zeal and abilities of many of the gentlemen who signed the address, for the success of several of the most important and useful measures of my Government, and that I shall consider myself fortunate if it should at any time be in my power to mark my personal regard for those individuals who have a particular claim to my esteem and gratitude, or to continue in any degree to promote the general prosperity of the British inhabitants of Calcutta.'

Shortly after this reply reached Bengal, the inhabitants of Calcutta were forwarding a congratulatory address to Warren Hastings on his final acquittal from the impeachment of Burke. Almost the last despatch of Cornwallis to the Court of Directors is dated from Madras in September, 1793. He tells them that on the Declaration of War against England and Holland by the French, he had taken immediate steps for the reduction of Pondicherry and the other French settlements, which had been crowned with success; and in all the bustle of departure, he finds time to address a letter of thanks to Sir John Shore, who had been his right hand and chief adviser. Cornwallis left Madras on the 10th of October, 1793, and he came to an anchor in the *Swallow* packet, in Torbay, on the 3rd of February, 1794. He had accomplished a great work in settling the land revenue system of Bengal on an intelligible basis. He had entirely changed the character of the Civil Service. He longed for a little peace and quiet; but there was still much work before him.

CHAPTER VI

The Perpetual Settlement of Benares

One of the immediate consequences of the introduction of the Perpetual Settlement into the Lower Provinces was its extension to the Province of Benares. This was accomplished by Sir John Shore, Cornwallis's successor. But the opinion formed by Cornwallis himself as to the state of the Province is so significant that it ought to be quoted. Writing in 1787, on two separate occasions, he delivers himself as follows:—

'Benares on its present system must be a scene of the grossest corruption and mismanagement. There could be no reason for not placing it under the Board of Revenue like other Zamíndárís, except the consideration of the Governor-General losing so much patronage. It would be better for the Zamíndár, the inhabitants, and the country, and will probably soon take place. I am not enough versed in all the secrets of Benares to enter into a minute detail of them at present. I propose, if no untoward circumstances happen to prevent it, to visit the upper Stations this year, and to set out at the end of July for that purpose. It will be material that I should get all possible information the first year.'

Again he writes:—

'Ill as I thought of the late system of Benares, I found it on enquiry much worse than I could have conceived. The Resident, although not regularly invested with any power, enjoyed the almost absolute government of the country without control. His emoluments, besides the thousand rupees per month allowed him by the Company, certainly amounted to little less than four lacks a year, exclusive of the complete monopoly of the whole commerce of the country, with the power of granting *parwánas*, &c. It has been generally supposed that in return for all these good things, the Residents at Benares have not been ungrateful to the friends of the Governor-General. I have no reason to suppose that Mr. —— *took* more than his predecessors—God knows what he *gave*; but as he was on bad terms with the Rájá and his servants, and as new measures are more likely to succeed with new men, I thought it better to remove him. Although many persons were desirous, nay even importunate, to show their zeal for the Company's service by undertaking this office, it was not very easy for me to find a successor to my mind. For I could not venture to lower the authority of the Resident too abruptly, from apprehension of losing our revenue; and as the Rájá is a fool, his servants rogues, every native of Hindustán (I really believe) corrupt, and Benares 600 miles from Calcutta, there was a danger, unless it was put into good hands, of the old system being in some degree continued.

'As I had the prosperity of Benares most exceedingly at heart, and as I felt that nothing could tend so much as a good management of that Province to raise our character and reputation in the remotest parts of Hindustán, I determined on this occasion to make a very great sacrifice, and, much against his own will, appointed Mr. Jonathan Duncan, the Secretary of the Public and Revenue departments, to that office. Perhaps you are not acquainted with Mr. Duncan's character: he is held in the highest estimation by every man, both European and native, in Bengal, and, next to Mr. Shore, was more capable of assisting me, particularly in revenue matters, than any man in this country. I am sorry to say that I have every reason to believe that at present almost all the Collectors are, under the name of some relation or friend, deeply engaged in commerce, and, by their influence as Collectors and Judges of Adálat, they become the most dangerous enemies to the Company's interest and the greatest oppressors of the manufactures. I hope you will approve of the additional allowances and the commission we have given to the Collectors, for without them it was absolutely impossible that an honest man could acquire the most moderate competency. After this liberality, I make no scruple in issuing the

Revenue regulations and orders against engaging in trade, which you will read, and I promise you that I will make an example of the first offender that I can catch.'

The development of the measure for the Permanent Settlement of Benares Province received the assent of Sir John Shore in March, 1795. From the laws and Regulations of 1795 there is good ground to infer that the measure had been adequately discussed and considered, and that the same prosperous results were looked for in the contentment of the landholders, the spread of agriculture, and the stability of the Government. Indeed, the Regulations of that time applicable to Benares, reveal a somewhat different state of things from what existed certainly in Lower Bengal, and to some extent in Behar; and they bristle with terms, titles, and phrases of a new kind, and provide for rights, interests, and customs of a cognate character to those of the Doáb of Hindustán. It seems that although a high official styled the Resident had been stationed at Benares before the year 1781, he had not been allowed to interfere in any way with the Settlement and collection of the revenue till the year 1787. The Rájá Mahip Náráyan, a nephew of the celebrated Chait Singh, administered the Province, with the aid of Náibs or deputies. In the last-mentioned year this duty was made over to the Resident, and he collected the dues of Government through functionaries styled

Aumils, whose position was analogous to those farmers in the Lower Provinces who were not Rájás or hereditary Zamíndárs. Settlements for one year and for five years were made through these functionaries.

Rules were laid down for the valuation of crops where the revenue was usually paid in kind by a division of the produce; for the consolidation of all extra cesses into one payment with the original rent; for the differences between the old and the new form of the measuring rod and the old and new *bíghás*, or portions of an acre; and for divers other matters calculated to remedy abuses, to prevent oppression, and to promote prosperity and peace. At the same time, it was provided that the Amils or farmers of the revenue were to look to the Zamíndárs or hereditary landholders for the realisation of the revenue; and here, for the first time in our revenue phraseology, we must interpret this familiar term to mean something very different from the high personages, whose estates might range from fifty villages to an extent of land of the size of an English county.

The local Zamíndár of Benares and the North-West Provinces signifies a sharer in an estate or village in which the whole land is held and managed in common. The rents, with all other profits from the estate, are thrown into a common stock, and after a deduction for all necessary expenses, the balance is divided among the proprietors according to their ancestral shares. The Zamíndár of Bengal and Behar, in fact, may somewhat loosely be described as a big, and the Zamíndár of the Upper Provinces as comparatively a small personage; and it would be also correct to say that the powerful Zamíndár in Bengal is analogous to the Tálukdár in Oudh.

It is quite clear that this distinction, though not fully expressed, was clearly understood and recognised by the administrators who framed the Perpetual Code for Benares on the model of that of 1793, and with just the necessary amplifications of the same, fitted to the special demands of the new Province. It seems also tolerably certain that the Permanent Settlement of Benares was preceded by enquiries of a more detailed and formal character than had been thought possible in Bengal Proper. Particulars of the assessment on the Tálukdárs and village Zamíndárs had been obtained; registers of lands exempted from payment of revenue, of pensions, and of charitable allowances, were drawn up. Recourse was had to local officers known as Kánúngos, and new forms of the documents known as *Pattás* and *Kabúliyats*, which are loosely termed leases and their counterparts, had been framed and issued under the authority of the Government. In order to facilitate the transition from a Settlement for five years to a Settlement in perpetuity, the English Resident and his Assistants made a regular tour throughout the Province in the cold season. They investigated the capabilities of the villages and of their divisions and subdivisions; provided for a restoration of their rights to some village Zamíndárs, as well as for the permanent exclusion of certain others who had been out of possession since July, 1775, the date of our acquisition of the Province; revised the assessments; arranged for a moderate and progressive increase of revenue from portions of lands found to be waste but culturable; took steps to prevent the levy of transit duties which had been abolished, and against the creation of new rent-free tenures: enforced the necessary stipulations for the maintenance of peace, the detection and communication of crime, and the restoration of stolen property. On the whole they proceeded with cautious local enquiries, which were a decided improvement on the summary proceedings of the Cornwallis administration on the one hand, but were yet much below the standard of the regular village Settlement, with its detailed record of rights, liabilities, and privileges, which on the other hand has been the glory of successive generations of officials of the school of Thomason in Upper India, and of Munro in Madras. Of course this was not accomplished without obstruction and the expenditure of trouble and time. It was discovered that the Amils, or farmers, had often availed themselves of their position and knowledge to 'procure deeds of conveyance[1], in their own names or those of their relations, for

[1] This objectionable practice is known as *ism-farzi* in the Upper and as *benámi* in the Lower Provinces.

lands the property of persons in arrears, whose balances had been wholly or partially liquidated.'

Local enquiries revealed the existence of serious disputes between *pattídárs*, or sharers in the same village, as to their respective portions and between different families claiming the same villages. As a rule the village Zamíndárs, either in actual occupancy or known to have been in possession at any time since the acquisition of the Province in 1775, were readmitted to Settlement; and while the Resident and his Assistants had power to fix the revenue payable, this ruling was to be no bar to the prosecution of any claim to a recovery of the proprietary right in the Civil Courts of the Province. In other words, the English revenue officer fixed the amount of revenue for each estate or village, and took an engagement from one out of two or more contending claimants before him. The amount of revenue could only be varied on appeal by the Resident or the Revenue Board.

A dissatisfied claimant for the Settlement was left to his new remedy before the civil tribunal; and if successful there, would succeed to his estate or village, burdened with the payment of the revenue already fixed. This amount the Civil Court had no power to vary. Divers other provisions with regard to certain Parganás or hundreds were included in the Regulation which is the land charter of the Province. They have reference to the services claims, and treatment of certain Rájás; to the rights of their tenant-proprietors; to certain villages held at quit-rents; and to other points which it is unnecessary here to specify in detail. It was roundly stated at the time that of the whole Province eight-twelfths were settled with the Zamíndárs; three-twelfths were still left in the hands of the Amils; and the remaining twelfth was, in the revenue phraseology, Amání[1]; that is to say, the revenue was neither farmed nor settled, but was collected by an official yearly, from each contributor direct; and it is indisputable from the language and style of the Regulations of this year that the administrators of the day had begun to recognise the existence of new and different tenures. The *pattídár*, or principal shareholder in a village, was admitted to engage in his own name for the payment of revenue, while those shareholders who were then styled inferior *pattídárs*, were 'annexed to or blended in common with the principal of the family,' or the head man of the cultivating brotherhood. But it was left optional with the inferior *pattídárs* to bring suits in the Civil Court for a separation of their family shares, and for the entry of their name in a distinct and separate engagement.

Village communities, if they ever existed in Bengal Proper, had disappeared when our rule began.

[1] Amání is elsewhere known as *Kham* or *Khás-tahsíl*. It may be terminated at the close of a year by the Collector and a Settlement made with some responsible person.

Certain villages and certain tracts of country were however found to be in the possession of particular castes. In one place the inhabitants were exclusively Muhammadan. Other villages and distinct *Mahallas*, or parts of villages, were tenanted wholly by fishermen, by weavers, or by the purely agricultural castes of Hindus—the Pōd, the Kaibart, the Kopali, and the Teor. But anything like an obligation to collect rents in common, apportion liabilities, and divide the surplus, it would not have been easy to find in Lower Bengal. There were numerous instances in which Bengalí Ryots combined to resist extortion, or to prevent a purchaser at auction or by private sale, or a lessor, from enforcing his legal rights. There were also the usual village functionaries and artisans necessary for agricultural occupations, *e.g.* the watchman, the carpenter, and the blacksmith. But of the co-parcenary tenure and the Bháyachára village occupied by the proprietary brotherhood, in which the revenue was assessed by a *bach* or rate, there was no trace at the acquisition of the Diwání in 1765, in Bengal Proper.

In several other matters, in spite of these variations in the landed tenures, the precedents of 1793 were closely followed. The exaction of tolls and taxes and duties was forbidden. Inland customs were to be levied at four towns only—Benares, Gh– ázípur, Juanpúr, and Mirzápur. The duties of the English Collector were specifically defined. He was to collect the revenue, whether due 'from Tálukdárs, Zamíndárs, and Pattídárs; or from estates farmed to Amils, or from estates in *amání*, for which no Settlement had been concluded. He was to endeavour to make a regular Settlement of estates of this latter class. His other functions, just as in Bengal Proper, were the payment of pensions, the management of estates under the Court of Wards, the due apportionment of revenue on estates that might be split in two or more parts, the collection of the excise, and the resumption of invalid rent-free tenures. Under the Collector were placed native Tahsíldárs, and minute rules were laid down for the issue by them of processes in case of defaulters, and for the eventual confinement of such persons.

Provisions were also made for the levy of fines, and in extreme cases for the forfeiture of the proprietary right. It is noteworthy that liberty to appeal against the proceedings of the revenue Collector to the Civil Court of the district, to the Provincial Court of Appeal, and to the Sadr, or highest Court, was expressly reserved to defaulting Tálukdárs and Zamíndárs. As in Bengal, so in Benares, the Governor-General in Council always contemplated the protection of all subordinate rights and interests in the land, and it is certain that this intention was carried out at an earlier period than was unfortunately the case in the Lower Provinces.

These rights were guarded in Benares by a distinct and separate law[1], and an equitable and comprehensive Regulation, known as VII of 1821, of which

[1] Reg. XXVII of 1795.

some notice may be taken hereafter, was passed for the enquiry into and Settlement of the rights and interests of all classes concerned with the land; and under this law adequate protection was afforded to Zamíndárs, Pattídárs, and others. Possibly, too, the sturdier character of the inhabitants of the Benares Province may have facilitated the task of Collectors and Settlement officers in this respect. The cultivators were more independent, and more ready to combine together for legitimate purposes of defence.

From whatever cause, it is certain that disturbances in regard to rents, exactions, and encroachments were less frequent, and the cause of less anxiety to our administrators in Benares, after it was thus permanently settled in 1795. The subsequent Settlement of the rights of tenant-proprietors, and Ryots generally, was the work of Collectors such as James Thomason in Azamgarh, and of others elsewhere under the admirable system devised by Robert Bird. It was accomplished gradually between 1832 and 1840, as far as the Province of Benares was concerned. To describe the regular Settlement of the Doáb of Hindustán and other districts in the North-West Provinces, by which the two names just mentioned have become household words to some twenty-five millions of Asiatics, forms no part of this memoir.

While the law for the punctual payment of revenue by the Zamíndárs of Bengal and Behar was enforced with stringency, and while defaulters were exposed to processes, confinement, and the eventual forfeiture of their rights, sufficient provision had not been made for the realisation of the Zamíndárs' rents, which are the basis of all land revenue. In 1793 a law had been enacted defining the extent of the legal coercion which landholders might exercise over under-farmers, dependent Tálukdárs, and Ryots, but it was soon found to be insufficient for this purpose; and in 1799 a further Regulation, No. VII, was enacted, which remained for more than half a century the principal statute relative to the recovery of arrears. By this law any tenant was considered a defaulter who withheld his rent beyond the day specified in his written engagement or, in default of specification, beyond the date sanctioned by local usage. The landholder was empowered to distrain crops and products of the earth, as well as cattle and other personal property. Ploughs and other implements of husbandry, cattle actually trained to the plough, and grain for seed, were exempted from attachment and sale, and the same protection was extended to lands, houses, and other immovable property. A notice of fifteen days was necessary before the attached property could be sold.

Further power was given to landholders to procure the arrest of dependent Tálukdárs, leaseholders, Ryots, or their sureties; and they were also authorised to summon, and if necessary to compel the attendance of their Ryots at their private Kacherí or local office, with the object of adjusting their balances, and of giving explanations in regard to delay in payment, or any other similar matter. This provision was very often grossly abused, and it was eventually abolished, to the dissatisfaction of the landholders, but to the effective relief of the Ryots, by a comprehensive statute in 1859. The decisions of these suits instituted for the recovery of rents were called summary suits.

The procedure was intended to be simple and expeditious. No arrear of more than one twelvemonth could be adjudged. And the power to hear such cases has, at various times, been shifted from the Civil Courts to the Collectors and back, so as to cause much perplexity and confusion. Rents that were due beyond the year could only be exacted by a regular civil suit. It is evident from the language of the whole law of 1799, which was intended to be very full and comprehensive, that many abuses had been already brought to light in the management of estates.

But it is by no means to be understood that Zamíndárs and their agents were always harsh and unscrupulous, or that the Ryot was invariably a down-trodden and innocent being. Instances could be quoted by scores in which both parties were in fault. If a Zamíndár was weak and inattentive to business and his agents careless, the Ryots could easily set him at defiance. When a new landlord came in by private purchase or public sale, it might take him six months or a year before he could realise any rent at all. The boundaries of his acquisition were ill-defined. Its area was uncertain. There were no maps, and the rent-roll, with the names of the tenants and their holdings, might not be available, or if found was often wanting in many important particulars. Frequently in sheer despair or from inability to manage a large estate, a Zamíndár would create a sub-infeudation on a part of it, or would grant a lease of the whole or half of his Zamíndárí to some determined and energetic Englishman.

In some cases the new owner or lessee found it necessary to bring a series of summary suits against defaulters, to measure lands under the protection of the police, and to institute a regular civil action to fix the rent according to the custom of the Parganá, on the different kinds of crops and lands, selecting for typical cases three or four of the most obstructive and substantial Ryots. In the end, a persevering landlord or lessee generally had his own way. Decrees were obtained, and after delays and appeals, were enforced against a head-man or permanent tenant-proprietor. The less determined villagers gave in, attended at the local office, and effected a private settlement; then, in all probability, the Zamíndár made up for lost time and money. He got what in Anglo-Indian phrase was termed the *dakhal*: that is to say, he obtained a firm footing in the village owing to command of means, knowledge of revenue practice, dexterity in management, and determination in carrying out his decrees. Rents were then punctually exacted. Ryots were compelled by force to attend at the Kacherí. Lands were measured and re-measured. Summary suits for the realisation of rents due in the year were followed by formidable regular suits brought to raise the old rent to the standard of the neighbourhood. In fact, by the machinery of the Courts and by pressure out of doors, a general all-round rise in rents was effected. In one district in Eastern Bengal the tenants were so distrustful of receipts and quittances given by agents, that they almost made it a rule to wait for the institution of a summary suit, when they at once paid the money into Court.

At other times it was not very easy to apportion the blame between a high-handed landlord and a defiant or obstructive Ryot. All that can be affirmed with absolute certainty is that no Ryots theoretically[1] ever objected to pay rent: that they combined equally for legitimate as for unlawful purposes: and that in the end it became the duty of the Government to interfere for their protection. And this eventually resulted in the well-known Act X of 1859. In the interim, the statutory provisions regarding the speedy realisation of rents were amended. The Preamble to Reg. V of 1812, passed in the administration of Lord Minto, is somewhat in the nature of an indictment against the Zamíndárs. There were grounds, it was deliberately said, for believing that this class had

[1] One exception may be made in the case of the Farází sect of Musalmáns in Eastern Bengal, who have at times propounded a theory that Hindus or infidels were not entitled to rent at all.

abused their powers and had been guilty of acts of oppression in connection with the distraint and sale of the property of their tenants. It was advisable to amend the law of distraint and to revise the rules for granting *pattás*, as well as those under which auction purchasers might collect their rents; and also to relieve defaulting Zamíndárs and farmers from a heavy penalty of twelve per cent. interest. It was therefore enacted that Zamíndárs were bound to serve their tenants with a written demand specifying the precise amount of their arrears. The notice was to be served personally on the tenant or affixed at his usual place of residence; and by way of relief or compensation the tenant, if he disputed the justice of the demand, was enabled to get the attachment taken off by making a certain application within five days and binding himself to institute a civil suit to contest the distraint and attachment within other fifteen days. But this provision was somewhat clogged with formalities, and in practice it was inoperative. The defaulting tenant had to execute a bond with a surety before either a Commissioner, a Judge, a Collector, or the Kází of the Parganá—a nondescript kind of functionary—that he would speedily institute his suit; and a civil suit in those days involved much trouble, a good deal of time, and no inconsiderable outlay.

If the suit was not instituted within the prescribed time, the attachment revived against the person and the property of the defaulter who had given sureties for his action, and the property of the unfortunate surety became liable for the arrears of rent, if no suit were brought. It is remarkable that in this law there is raised for the first time a doubt as to the existence of any regular standard known as the Parganá Rates. Failing such rates, rents were to be assessed and collections made according to the rates payable for lands of a similar description in the neighbourhood. There was another not unimportant section by which an enhanced rate of rent could not be levied or awarded judicially unless the tenant had been served with a formal notice of enhancement during the month of Jeth or Jyeshtha. This date corresponds with the latter half of May and the beginning of June, and is always regarded as the link between one agricultural year and another. Agricultural operations, which are either suspended or languidly pursued in May, recommence after the beginning of the periodical rains; and this event occurs about the second week of June in Bengal, and towards the end of that month or at the beginning of July in Behar.

Of the excellent intentions of the framers of this law there can be no doubt. Remedies were always provided in every Regulation dealing with landlord and tenant, for redress against the injustice of summary decisions by referring discontented parties to the Civil Court. But, as has been already said, procedure in those Courts was then cumbrous and slow. Resort was had to them more by the landlord than by the tenant, and though Ryots were brought to understand the simple procedure of a summary suit before either the Collector or the Civil Judge, and were not backward in applying to the magistrate for advice and protection, it may be fairly questioned whether a real redress for his grievances was provided till nearly sixty years after the administration of Cornwallis.

In 1859, the Legislative Council, constituted by Lord Dalhousie in 1854, passed an Act which has been termed the Magna Charta of the Ryots.

CHAPTER VII

MADRAS. SALE LAWS. RESUMPTIONS

THE introduction of the Permanent Settlement into the Province of Benares seems, from the legislative and official correspondence of the time, to have followed rather as a matter of course. But the Court of Directors inclined to the opinion that the same measure might be introduced into the Madras Presidency, as they were sensible 'of the propriety and expediency of the late revenue and judicial regulations established in Bengal.' A vast amount of correspondence ensued. Both the Madras and the Bombay Governments had been furnished by Cornwallis with all the papers regarding the Bengal Settlement and the establishment of the new Courts of justice. The Revenue Board at Madras directed an elaborate enquiry into the resources of certain tracts which at that time, or about 1798–9, comprised Báránahal and Dindigal, Coimbatore and Kánara, a district subsequently transferred to Bombay. Much caution had been enjoined and information had been procured of the various Collectors about the rights of the under-tenants and other proprietors. A comprehensive report was eventually sent home, and about the year 1802 a Special Commission was appointed to settle permanently the land revenue of those parts of the Madras Presidency for which sufficient materials had been collected.

Within two years the Permanent Settlement was introduced into the Northern Circárs, and by 1806–7 the following districts were settled on the same plan. A Jaghír obtained from the Nawáb of Arcot in 1750 and 1763, which surrounds the Presidency town, and is now Chengalpat; later acquisitions, including the districts of Salem; several tracts termed Pollams held by powerful turbulent chiefs, known as Polygars; Rámnád, Krishnagiri, and some others of less importance, were all included in the same category. But at this very time other views began to prevail. In some places the fixed revenues had been collected with greater facility. But in the Jaghír, which had been converted into a Collectorate, the revenue had not been paid with punctuality. Certain estates had been sold for default, and some others had been thrown back on the hands of Government. Part of the failure was due to a calamitous season, but serious mistakes had been made in estimating the rents of the tenants, or in fixing the assessment of the Zamíndárs, and a formidable rival to the supporters of a Permanent Settlement appeared in the person of Thomas Munro. He showed conclusively that a Settlement made with individual proprietors, though apparently intricate and laborious, had been familiar to native Governments; that individuals called Patels, or head-men, were perfectly capable of aiding in the Settlement of their respective villages; that a complete establishment of hereditary revenue servants was already in existence; that Ryots were in the habit of meeting and holding discussions about agricultural stock, cultivation, and payment of rent; and that an active Collector making the circuit of his district, and beginning when the early crop was reaped and the late crop sown, was quite capable of conducting these multifarious operations to an issue financially profitable to Government, and socially advantageous to the Ryot. There was more correspondence of the usual kind; statistics, reports, Minutes, and Resolutions. In the end, the Permanent Assessment was staid. In only a single portion of the Madras Territory had the Bengal system been introduced. Malabar, Kánara, Coimbatore, the Ceded Districts, Nellore and Arcot, and those magnificent tracts of country comprised in Tanjore, Trichinopoli, and Tinnevelli had nearly all escaped.

This is not the place to discuss minutely the merits and demerits of the various revenue systems prevailing in different provinces of India. Variety in the mode of collecting the dues of the State, and in the persons or communities responsible for the revenue, is an essential part of our administration, and contributes to the accumulation of a large stock of experience. The error in Bengal was that, from a variety of causes, the corollary to a new and comprehensive measure which had established a solid landed aristocracy, was not carried out for more than half a century. In the greater part of Madras the settlement is Ryotwárí, and though in cases where Zamíndárs have thrown up their estates, and Government has stepped in, the Ryotwárí system has been introduced, the converse operation has never taken place. No district and no part of a district put under the Ryotwárí system, has ever again reverted to the Zamíndárs.

The multifarious and important sub-infeudations which have arisen out of Cornwallis's Zamíndárí system may claim a little attention. Although reliable statistics in regard to trade, commerce, agriculture, and population have only been collected of very late years, there are the broad facts in regard to the Lower Provinces in general, and to Eastern and Central Bengal in particular, which have been so prominent as to admit of no dispute. The alluvial soil was extremely fertile and the revenue assessment was light. For some years, as has been shown, the Zamíndárs were restricted from giving perpetual leases of villages or portions of their estates. But it soon became clear that whatever laws Government might enact for the benefit of the cultivators and for the security of its own exchequer, the Zamíndár could not be prevented from assigning to other persons those distinct rights which had been vested in him as superior landlord. He very soon turned this undeniable privilege into a source of profit. Sometimes the Zamíndárí was unwieldy and large. Ryots were obstinate and difficult to manage. Servants were corrupt and untrustworthy. The Zamíndár had become involved in expensive litigation, or he wanted funds to dedicate a temple, to marry a son or daughter, to entertain a host of Bráhmans at a Sráddha or sacrificial supper, to build a new residence, to satisfy the caprice of the moment, the duty of charity, and the obligations of religion.

The Mahárájá of Bardwán, whose descendants are still amongst the most opulent of the Bengal landholders, had been in the habit of creating sub-tenures known as Patni. In its etymological meaning this word signified a Settlement or colony. In revenue phraseology it came to designate a Táluk created by the Zamíndár on the whole or a part of his estate, 'to be held at a rent fixed in perpetuity by the lessee and his heirs for ever[1].' The Patanidár practically stepped into the place of the Zamíndár who, though in theory still held bound by the Government to discharge his obligations, to aid the police, and to report crimes, became practically a rent-charger on this portion of his estate. The Patanidár having paid a considerable sum as bonus for the creation of his own title, acquired a permanent estate with the

[1] Regulation VIII of 1819.

right of sale and transfer, and all the other privileges of his lessor. By the law of 1819 arrears of Patni rent could be exacted by the Zamíndár, not merely by the ordinary process of a suit, but by the summary process of sale by the Collector after due notice, and the execution of certain formalities. The Zamíndár's estate, when in default, was liable to be put up to public auction at four stated periods of the year. That of the Patanidár could be sold only at two periods—in the month of May and in October.

Rules were passed in the same law cancelling all subordinate creations in the event of such public auction, and yet allowing the holders of the incumbrances to save their properties by depositing the amount of arrears claimed by the superior landlord. Generally speaking, the new law gave validity to a series of transactions which, originating in Bardwán, had been followed by the landholders of other districts and had by degrees spread over the whole country.

So far, in all probability, the creation of Patnis, or rather the sub-division of large estates into what is really a separate estate more compact and manageable, might have worked well. The public revenue was safeguarded. The condition of the tenant proprietor would not have been impaired. But, unfortunately, the practice commenced by the Zamíndár was improved and extended by his creation, the Patanidár. He, in his turn, harassed by contests with his Ryots, or requiring a round sum to be paid down for his own convenience, parted with his rights and privileges as a Patanidár of the second degree, and the latter to another of the third degree. These latter creations were termed Dar-Patanidárs and Seh-Patanidárs.

It is useless now, after the lapse of sixty years, to discuss the policy of giving statutory effect to these repeated devolutions of duties and rights, or to enquire whether it would not have been both fair and equitable to have recognised the creation of the first incumbrance and nothing beyond. But what is undeniable is, that as each Patanidár of the first, second, and third degree, looked for some profit over and above the ordinary rental of the village, the burden of creating and supplying such excess fell on the actual cultivators. It was not likely that a Patanidár of any class would assume the position of a mere rent-collector satisfied with a small commission as his only reward. The law already quoted vested the Patanidár with the right of sub-letting the Táluks 'in the manner they might deem most conducive to their own interest,' and the legislators of that day directed their attention rather to the security of the public revenue and to the privileges of the Zamíndár than to the protection of the Ryot.

Patnis were for a long time the only under-tenures on behalf of which fresh legislation was particularly demanded. But many varieties of similar tenures, known by different names and held under varying conditions, were created all over the province. In the district of Bákarganj there were found four and five of such sub-infeudations interposed between the landholder and the cultivating tenant. They were repeatedly the subject of judicial investigation and had the sanction of decrees of Court. They were alluded to, if not definitely protected, in the various laws passed to regulate sales of land for arrears of revenue, and facilities were given to the holders of such under-tenures to register their holdings specially, so as to protect them from cancelment in the event of the sale of the superior right. That there has been found for nearly a century a margin of profit for tenures intervening three and four deep between the Zamíndár and the Ryot; that the jungle has diminished; that agriculture has spread; that a magnificent internal trade has sprung up; that fleets of country boats, lines of bullock-carts, and thousands of miles of railway, have been required for the transport of produce of every description to centres of internal commerce as well as to the port of Calcutta; is due in part to natural causes operating on a soil of unrivalled fertility, renewed in many places by the silt deposits of a thousand streams, but also to the patient industry and steady cultivation of the Ryot, who knows how to make the most of the capacity of his holding, and with primitive instruments as ancient as the days of Asoka or Manu has produced astonishing, if 'unscientific,' results.

It has not always been easy to define the limits of

an under-tenure by any precise form of words, or to say when a tenant-proprietor of the substantial class who has cultivating tenants under him, ought to be reckoned as the holder of a sub-tenure. Recently an attempt has been made to separate the two classes and give them a distinct statutory recognition. Practically, a district officer who knows his business would have little difficulty in coming to a decision as to the status of any one individual case.

The Sale Laws of Bengal affixing the penalty of loss and cancelment of an estate to a failure to pay the revenue at the specified times, have often been treated as if they were inexorable and harsh. They have not seldom been modified between 1793 and 1859. But their effect has been to secure punctuality of payment—which could not have been secured by any other means—and to protect the claims of Government, without, of recent years, inflicting any real injury on the Zamíndárs as a class. Doubtless at the commencement of this century, when estates were put up to sale at Calcutta only and not in the several districts where they were situated, without sufficient notice, and much oftener than once a quarter, many estates were sold in haste and purchased by speculators or persons interested in concealing facts from the owners. But for the last fifty years provisions have been introduced which have simplified and mitigated the law. Persons having a lien on the estate are allowed to pay up the sum necessary to preserve it from sale. A sharer is protected against the wilful or careless default of a co-sharer.

Sales are conducted with due formalities, of which all interested parties have notice; and though a sale is in theory held to annul all incumbrances, to vest the purchaser with what is analogous to a Parliamentary title, and to allow him to enter on a clear property not clogged or fettered by the acts or imprudence of his predecessor, it has been thought expedient to preserve from cancelment not only certain old under-tenures and Ryots with rights of occupation, but other interests which have grown up in the general development and progress of the Province. Lands held at *bonâ-fide* leases at fair rents, or let in farms for periods not exceeding twenty years, were exempted. And in the former class were included mines, gardens, manufactures, tanks, canals, places of worship, and burying-grounds. It may be safely said that during the last half-century and more no valuable estates have come to the hammer by the mere operation of the law of arrears and sale. Many miserable properties have been bought for Government at a small or a nominal sum, in default of any private bidders, and the management of these properties, termed 'Khás Mahals,' or 'private estates,' forms a distinct and special branch of the duties of every Collector. The Government, in such cases, has acquired the Zamíndárí as well as the Sovereign right.

These State-purchases are generally farmed out to some enterprising individual, who is often an Englishman, and it has lately been calculated that the whole yearly revenue derivable from this source in the Lower Provinces does not amount to much more than £220,000 a year—a sum insignificant in comparison with the rent-roll of other landed gentry all over the Province. On this part of the subject it may be safely asserted that the economic result of the land laws for Bengal; of the tendency of the joint Hindu family system to sub-divide and separate estates; of the inevitable increase of population, wealth, and capital, derived from commerce, banking, and enterprise; of the desire of new men to possess old acres; and of the general sense of security created by nearly a century of peace; is one which Cornwallis in a certain measure anticipated, and which he would have rejoiced to see.

On another division of this subject, the action taken by Government was not satisfactory. At all times and in all provinces of India, its rulers have been in the habit of making grants of land, to be held free from the payment of revenue, to Bráhmans and priests, for the endowment of places of worship; to men who had done good service in civil and military capacities; and to favourites of every conceivable degree of merit or demerit—ministers, fiddlers, dancing-girls, concubines, buffoons, soothsayers, and cooks. Warren Hastings was fully aware of the existence of these grants; and Cornwallis had, as has been seen, contemplated an early enquiry into the validity of the titles by which they were held. Unfortunately, each Governor-General from Cornwallis to Bentinck was also Governor of Bengal, and had his hands fully occupied with wars and conquests, the cession and pacification of new territories, and the enactment of legislative measures of paramount necessity or undisputed advantage. Thus, although divers discussions took place, and though a special law for the resumption of illegal and invalid tenures was passed during the administration of the Marquess of Hastings, in 1819, nothing was done till ten further years had elapsed.

It was, beyond any doubt, a fundamental principle of the Settlement of Bengal, and indeed of that of every province in India, that the Ruling Power was entitled to some portion of the produce of every acre of land, unless that same power had waived or alienated its rights for a time or in perpetuity, and by the grant of title-deeds or documents which the British Government would be bound to respect. So in 1828 a class of officers, termed Special Commissioners, was called into existence to enquire into these alienations, and subsequently there were placed under them others, designated Special Deputy Collectors, each of whom had charge of this department of enquiry in three or four districts, and whose duties were kept distinct from those of the ordinary Collectors. The alienations were at first divided into two broad classes. Those which had been granted by the Sovereign or Emperor, which were known as Bádsháhi or Royal grants, and those which had been conferred by rulers of provinces, Viceroys, Zamíndárs or Amils, and other high functionaries. These latter were known as Húkmi grants. The highest form of these alienations was that of Altumgha, or the great seal. Another description was known as Madad-i-maish, or 'in aid of subsistence.' The villages said to have been assigned by the Persian monarch to Themistocles must have been of this sort. Then there were various other descriptions: Devattar, grants for temples; Brahmattar to Bráhmans; Mahattrán to the Súdra caste; Aima, lands given in charity and held at a quit-rent; Pírán and Fakirán, lands given to Muhammadan saints or their shrines, and to Fakirs; and several others. In order to avoid minute and harassing enquiries, it was ruled that all grants less than one hundred *bíghás* in extent were to be exempt from investigation, and this exemption was subsequently extended to parcels of land of less than fifty *bíghás* each, though one or more such parcels might be covered by one Farmán or Sannad, and might in the aggregate amount to more than one hundred *bíghás*.

But the excitement which the Resumption Laws caused in the native community was excessive and was not soon forgotten. In the course of half a century, many of the original title-deeds had disappeared:

ruined by damp, eaten by insects, destroyed in the fires which break out in the dry season in every bázár, and reduce the whole place to ashes in a couple of hours. The temptation to replace the missing deeds by forging new ones was irresistible.

Again, many of the lands originally granted for support of religious foundations and to pious and learned persons, had been sold or diverted to secular purposes. Many, like the kingdoms which had 'overset and passed from hand to hand,' had also changed hands. The native community had been lulled into a false security while Government was sleeping over its own rights. For months and years a violent controversy raged in the press, in which the partisans of the Government and the advocates of the Lákhirájdár displayed remarkable ability and ingenuity.

In the progress of the enquiry, various concessions were made by the Government to remove some of the discontent. Resumption was not insisted on, if the purposes for which the grant had been made originally were still carried out; if there were strong presumption that they were of a date anterior to 1765, or the Diwání; and if there were proof of continuous and uninterrupted possession subsequent to that date. The effect of these investigations was in Bengal to increase the Government revenue by about thirty-eight lacks a year, the whole operations having cost one hundred and twenty lacks. But a vast number of small portions of land, which had been expressly excluded from the claims of the Government, were still left exposed to the assessment of the Zamíndárs.

As the onus for proving his Lákhiráj, or rent-free title, was properly placed on the Ryot claiming it, many of these titles were challenged in the Courts of law, and, when found to be defective, were declared liable to assessment of rent. All over Bengal, however, there are still to be found examples of Devattar and Brahmattar, and other descriptions of land which have escaped the ordeal; and there is a sort of understanding amongst the community that Ryots who cultivate such lands for their fortunate possessors are entitled to sit at lower rents than the tenants of an ordinary Táluk or Jot. Warned by the excitement moved by such resumptions, the Indian Government, in all its later acquisitions of conquest or cession, has been more expeditious in the assertion of its rights. The enquiry has been made as soon as circumstances permitted, on well-considered principles, and with a leaning towards the intentions of the grantors. In some instances the grant has been prolonged for two and three generations, and then has been assessed at half-rates. There can be no doubt that in every province such grants, made by one dynasty, ruler, or Viceroy, were understood to be subject to the goodwill and pleasure of the successor. The just and equitable policy is for the revenue department to overhaul all these alienations at the time when the regular settlement—whether Tálukdárí, village community, or Ryotwárí—is carried out. To separate the two operations, and to postpone the Lákhiráj enquiry, was an error in the eyes of natives, almost equivalent to resumption by the strong hand of a despot.

In carrying out other administrative measures, which followed on the Cornwallis Code, something of the same laxity was apparent. The quinquennial registers contemplated by the laws of 1793 and 1800, and intended to show the changes in estates and in their owners, were never properly kept up. New shareholders and purchasers were allowed to register their names on the Collector's rent-roll, or not—just as they chose. The local officials, known as Kánúngoes and Patwárís, the latter being village accountants who in other parts of India keep up the statistics of the villages, gradually disappeared. In another direction something was at last done. A field survey of the Province was thought impolitic, owing to its enormous expanse. But a survey of the Mahals, or estates, was begun by the revenue officers some forty years ago; and this rough survey, as it was termed, was tested and verified by another set of officers, chiefly of the staff corps, who used a more accurate set of instruments and had more technical skill. Much information was collected in this way. Accurate lists of villages were made; maps were drawn of estates in blocks, and where—as was often the case—one single village was parcelled out amongst different estates, crossing and re-crossing each other in detached portions, the maps were proportionately minute, accurate, and detailed. All natural and all remarkable artificial objects were entered on the maps; tanks and rivers, depressions and *nullahs*, mosques and temples, residences of stone and brick.

A considerable amount of agricultural and commercial statistics was collected. Thus the geographical features, the character of the rivers, the staple crops and other products of the land, the flora and fauna, the trades and castes, the existing facilities for communication by land and water, the principal wholesale marts, and divers other local characteristics, were duly investigated, reported on, and published.

These enquiries were for the most part instituted without offending prejudice or creating or exciting groundless fear about enhancement of taxation. It has been said that if it were worth while to incur expense and depute two different sets of officials to survey the land—first with the prismatic compass, and then with the theodolite, it would have been politic, advantageous, and easy to extend the character and broaden the aims of the enquiry. With a little more expense, the survey might have included the complete demarcation of *mouzahs* or villages, in the revenue sense of the term, and even of fields and plots.

But in Lower Bengal, more perhaps than in any other Province of India, the most unexpected changes are wrought by the tremendous force of its streams, bringing down a yellow flood in the rainy season. A vast body of water cuts through natural obstacles; sweeps away whole villages; corrodes and absorbs half or the whole of an estate; inundates large tracts, and disappears in the month of October, to leave behind it a fresh alluvial soil, from which every familiar landmark has disappeared, while bewildered owners make vague guesses at the outline of their former possessions, and the most experienced boatman anchors his craft at an unfamiliar landing-place and launches it on a new stream. Nor is it superfluous to remark that the whole community of Bengal Proper has for nearly a century been accustomed to be governed by the action of the judicial Courts. Settlement officers, native Tahsíldárs, and all the admirable machinery so familiar in other Provinces, have there never sprung into life; and if Courts of first instance have of late years been multiplied, if new districts have been created, and facilities for the disposal of revenue and criminal cases been multiplied by the formation of sub-divisions, it may be asked whether some of the objects of the Cornwallis Settlement have not at last been fully attained.

That the Perpetual Settlement should have been put forward to support groundless claims and justify unfair exemptions which no ruler could grant, was to be expected. It has been invoked as a guarantee against the imposition of new forms of taxation, imperial and local. It was humorously said by a very able Lieutenant-Governor of Bengal, that at one time jealousy of any enquiry prevailed to such an extent that to ask any Ryot his name, except in a Court of justice, was tantamount to a violation of the rights of landlords. And the liability of the Zamíndárs to contribute to the calls of the State by taxation other than an increase of their land assessment, was thoroughly discussed and decided by the Secretary[1] of State for the time, some twenty years ago. The guarantee of 1793, it was clearly reasoned, only affected the land revenue. Zamíndárs could not be exempted from the other calls to which every subject is liable, without unduly increasing the burdens of less favoured classes in Bengal and in other Provinces. But the Perpetual Settlement of the land cannot be altered or impaired. It is still remembered with the gratitude due to its author. It has committed the British nation to pledges from which no Viceroy can think of drawing back.

[1] The Duke of Argyll.

CHAPTER VIII

Mission to the Continent. Indian Correspondence

Cornwallis was not long permitted to enjoy the rest to which in India he had often looked forward and which he had fairly earned. Kaye writes very happily that the Ministry of the day regarded the ex-Governor-General not as one who had been employed for the good of his country in the East, but as one who was still to be employed for his country's good in the West. An English army had been sent to Flanders to co-operate with the Austrians, Prussians, and Dutch in the defence of that country. The Duke of York, who commanded the English army, had defeated Pichegru. The Austrians, under Generals Clerfait and Kaunitz, had experienced a severe check.

The Austrian and Prussian generals held very different views about the employment of the Allied Army, and in order to mediate between them and to obviate jealousy and discontent, Cornwallis, within four months of his return from India, was sent on a mission to Flanders to explain matters to the Emperor of Austria. He was not given a very definite position or command, but it was soon obvious that his deputation meant, practically, the supersession of the Duke of York, and eventually Cornwallis felt himself compelled to address a letter to his Royal Highness explanatory of the motives which had led him to accept the mission. It is creditable to the Duke that he took in good part the manly and straightforward explanation which was entirely in accordance with the character and motives of Cornwallis, at every critical conjuncture. Pitt and Dundas, it is tolerably clear, would have favoured a plan for giving Cornwallis the rank of Field Marshal, and virtually placing him in command of the entire allied force. But there were insurmountable difficulties in the way. The Austrians did not want the Prussians to act on the Meuse, but required them in West Flanders, and they deprecated the exposure of the Rhine boundary to the attacks of the French. Mällendorf, the Prussian general, on the other hand, refused to respond to a request for any such employment of his troops in Flanders, and after divers conferences and much correspondence, the plan of putting Cornwallis at the head of the combined forces was abandoned, and he returned to England sometime in the middle of 1794.

He was, however, still consulted by the Ministry about the conduct of operations on the Continent. Cornwallis recognised the necessity for acting on the offensive, for the employment of a considerable English force, and for a Commander-in-Chief of capacity and resolution. Engaged as he was in matters of paramount importance to the influence of England at Continental Courts, he had still time to devote to news from India, and we get occasional glimpses of his private life. He took a house in Lower Grosvenor Street from Lord Hertford, completely furnished, for which he paid 600 guineas a year. He purchased a manor and estate adjoining the park of Lord Bristol for £12,000, and he was only prevented from giving evidence on the impeachment of Warren Hastings, at the solicitation of the accused, by an attack of illness. Afterwards, however, his evidence was taken by the managers.

Early in 1795 Cornwallis was made Master of the Ordnance, a post which he would gladly have exchanged for the Tower, and this was soon afterwards followed by the command of the troops in Essex and Hertfordshire, with head-quarters at Warley. Owing to the disturbed state of the Continent, his command was one of responsibility and importance, for he had under him no fewer than two lieutenant-generals and five major-generals. But Indian affairs were perpetually engaging his attention. Shore writes to him about the death of Sindia, and the Royal and Company's troops. General Abercromby tells him that at Shore's bidding he had to put down a rising promoted by Ghulám Muhammad, a young son of the deceased Nawáb of Rámpur. Cornwallis found time to answer Shore, and to give to another correspondent a memorandum in which the jurisdiction of the Supreme Courts of the Presidencies over any natives is very strongly deprecated. Attempts made at various periods of Indian history to extend the authority of the old Supreme Court to natives not residing within the limits of the Presidency towns, have been frustrated.

But Cornwallis seems to have gone further, and to have recommended that litigation in the Presidency Courts should be confined to cases in which both the litigants were Englishmen, or at any rate were not natives. He was of opinion that natives, under proper safeguards, might be summoned before such Courts as witnesses only. But what he dreaded was the expensive character of such litigation and the subjection of Asiatics to the jurisdiction of tribunals that administered strange laws in a language which, at that time, few natives could understand.

Controversies on this and similar points, and as to whether Englishmen in their turn should or should not be subjected to the local tribunals in civil and criminal cases, have at various times convulsed Anglo-Indian society. Such agitation was not set at rest till the amalgamation of the Supreme and Sadr Courts of the Presidency into one tribunal, styled the High Court, in 1862. The fusion was due to the able and constructive statesmanship of the late Lord Halifax. But it is interesting to observe how Cornwallis had anticipated that this question of jurisdiction, whether of English Courts over natives, or of local tribunals over Englishmen engaged in mercantile pursuits in the interior of the country, was sure to provoke a vehement discussion.

India was, however, at the end of the last century destined to be the scene of an agitation far more dangerous to our supremacy and one which threatened the very foundation of our power. Cornwallis had circulated some queries about the Royal and the Company's troops to thirteen distinguished officers, most of whom were in the Company's service. This enquiry got wind, and it was taken up, on imperfect knowledge and in an adverse sense, by Englishmen serving in the native regiments. Officers met, appointed delegates, swore each other to secrecy, and formulated proposals subversive of all discipline, and to speak plainly, characterised by amazing effrontery. The delegates insisted that the Royal troops should never exceed a small fixed number; that generals in the King's army should be ineligible for staff appointments; that all promotions should go by seniority; and that no general officer should ever be *selected* for a command.

There were other demands equally offensive and incompatible with discipline. Sir John Shore at Calcutta was so perturbed at the spectacle of this insubordination that he wanted troops to be sent from the Cape of Good Hope and Madras to awe the officers into submission, and he warned Lord Keith that the naval force under his command might be called up to Calcutta. The Ministry at home were evidently perplexed, and Dundas in a letter of entreaty begged Cornwallis to bring himself to forego the comforts of home for one year, and to proceed to India to settle the claims of the officers. Dundas held rightly that the very British Empire might be at stake, and he was even prepared, had Cornwallis refused the appointment, to proceed to India himself.

But Dundas had a firm belief that all difficulties would vanish on the mere mention of the name of Cornwallis. Cornwallis actually consented to go, and in one of his many confidential letters to General Ross he briefly says, 'The die is cast, and I am to go out to India: how sorry I feel that your domestic circumstances put it out of my power to ask you to accompany me.' Events, however, then took another turn. Some of the loyal Bengal officers repudiated the pretensions of the delegates. Concessions were made by the Board of Control and by the Court of Directors which did not at all commend themselves to Cornwallis. Indeed he calls one of his proposed instructions 'a milk-and-water order.' A mutiny broke out at Portsmouth, and Cornwallis gave up his appointment to India in August, 1797.

His services were next required much nearer home, in a position which has tried and been fatal to the reputation of many men whose claims to statesmanship are recognised, and which from the violence of parties, the clash of interests, the exposure to relentless and searching criticism that follows immediately on action, was at that special period calculated to test all the qualities of firmness, decision, tact, and constructive statesmanship. It was as trying as a campaign against an Oriental usurper, as the purification of the Indian service, or as the establishment of a land tax on a new basis. Lord Camden was about to relinquish his post as Lord-Lieutenant of Ireland, and the Ministry determined to replace him by Lord Cornwallis as Viceroy and Commander-in-Chief. It does not come within the scope of this memoir to give even a summary of the administration which preceded the Union. Cornwallis assumed his onerous and responsible office in June, 1798, and was succeeded by Lord Hardwicke in May, 1801. In these three years the Union was carried out.

Amidst all the anxieties, disappointments, crosses and vexations by which Cornwallis was tried during his Irish administration, it is pleasant to turn to his Indian correspondence. The Viceroy of Ireland had never forgotten the Governor-General of India. He had naturally been much interested and alarmed by the insubordination of the officers of the Bengal army; and just after hearing of the suppression of the delegates and the triumph of the loyal and faithful officers, he had been asked or had volunteered to give to an officer proceeding to India a letter of introduction to Sir John Shore, his successor in the Governor-Generalship. It is brief, and must be reproduced with only a word of explanation.

'Whitehall, June 10th, 1796.

'To Sir John Shore.

'Dear Sir,

'I beg leave to introduce to you Colonel Wesley (*sic*), who is Lieutenant-colonel of my regiment. He is a sensible man and a good officer, and will, I have no doubt, conduct himself in a manner to merit your approbation.'

The bearer of the letter was Arthur Wellesley, afterwards Duke of Wellington.

To the claims of another officer whose name is not given, Cornwallis turns a deaf ear. Dundas was pressed to nominate to the Madras Council a civil servant of whom Cornwallis knew a little too much. It was not prudent, he says, to charge him with corruption which could not be proved, though it was strongly suspected; but in a letter to Dundas it is shown that the appointment of a suspected intriguer would be highly inexpedient. The whole administration of Madras at that period required a more thorough reform than Bengal. Another letter about a young man, a member of Parliament who was proceeding to India, not in any official situation, might have been written with effect at the present day.

'As Mr. —— is a member of Parliament, he may be looked up to by the young men of the Settlement, who have chiefly gone abroad at a very early period of life, and are conseouently very ill-informed in regard to European politics. Nothing could be so prejudicial to themselves as well as to the general good order of the Settlement as to instil into their minds a spirit of party and of opposition to all government. Liberty and equality is a most pernicious and dangerous doctrine in all parts of the world; but it is particularly ill-suited to the Company's servants in India, who are to thrive by minding their own business and paying a due regard to the commands of their superiors in the service.'

In April, 1799, when the resistance to the Union of Ireland was most felt, Cornwallis sincerely repents that he did not return to Bengal. In July he gets a letter from the Marquess of Wellesley, then Lord Mornington, who had succeeded Sir John Shore, giving an account of the assassination of Mr. Cherry at Benares in an émeute got up by the partisans of Vizir Alí. This news filled him with sorrow, but a few months afterwards a mail from India caused him much gratification. After the final storming of Seringapatam, in May 1799, the army voted an address to the late Commander-in-Chief, who had carried on two campaigns against Tipú. The officers presented him with the turban of the deceased ruler and the sword of a Maráthá chief. It was brought to England by General Harris, great-grandfather of the present Governor of Bombay (1890).

It is amusing to find Cornwallis's old-standing and strong dislike to Madras re-appearing in his disapproval of the plan of annexing Malabar to the Presidency. He would not, however, stir in the matter. Dundas at the India Board was jealous of any interference with his own department, and there was quite enough of controversial matters in Ireland without any addition from Indian disputes and claims. It may be mentioned while keeping clear of the Irish controversy, that just as Cornwallis was about to leave, the Ministry had received information from another quarter about a supposed conspiracy and an intended massacre. It is characterised by Cornwallis as a great exaggeration, and the Duke of Portland is recommended to accept with a degree of qualification stories circulated in England regarding the state of Ireland. The following extracts show the exact state of his feelings on retirement from office [1]:—

'The joy that I should feel at being released from a situation which, with regard to every idea of enjoyment of life, has been most irksome to me, will be greatly alloyed by my apprehension that I am leaving a people who love me, and whose happiness I had so nearly secured in a state of progressive misery.'

Three days afterwards he writes to another friend: —'You know me too well to doubt my being happy at the thoughts of retirement, and you will likewise believe that the ungracious circumstances that attend it do not give me much concern, but the reflection of

[1] Major-General Ross. May 12th, 1801.

the misery to which a people are doomed who have shown me every mark of gratitude and affection, and the ultimate danger to which the convulsions in Ireland will expose the British Empire, are a severe alloy to my prospects of future enjoyment.'

On the 25th of May Lord Hardwicke had arrived at Dublin and succeeded Cornwallis. On the 28th Cornwallis was at Holyhead. On the 30th he writes from Shrewsbury that the roads and the weather were so bad that he cannot think of attempting to perform the journey between that town and London in two days. His Irish administration had been to him a sore trial. His return to England was a release and not a triumph. He had expressed a wish to retire from his situation, and the Ministry had taken him at his word. Still followed by correspondents in Ireland who claimed the fulfilment of alleged promises and worried for recommendations to Lord Hardwicke, Cornwallis was glad to get to Culford and to enjoy the society of his son, his daughter-in-law, and their two children. Here his time was taken up with letters about Indian taxation, which he says was loosely mentioned in Minutes and papers written at the time of the Permanent Settlement. 'It (the imposition of other taxes) must be exercised with great prudence and discretion, and must not be left to the capricious will of the Governor. It has the disadvantage of novelty, which is a very serious one in a country so bigoted to old habits.' His repose was soon disturbed by the offer of the command of the Eastern district.

Cornwallis would have preferred an order to go to Egypt, but always responding to the call of duty, he took up his post at Colchester 'without horses, house, or aide-de-camp.' The forces at his disposal were not more than eight weak regiments of militia, 'making about 2800 firelocks,' and two regiments of dragoons. His very natural fears for the safety of the country were somewhat allayed by the sight of two line-of-battle ships and a 74 *razée* (cut down) stationed near Clackton Beach and Walton Tower. 'In our wooden walls alone must we place our trust. We should make a sad business of it on shore;' and then he indulges in a hit at some evidently incompetent military officer. 'If it is really intended that —— should defend Kent and Sussex, it is of very little consequence what army you place under his command.' In the month of August the public fear of invasion began to subside. In the month of September, however, Cornwallis was still full of anxiety. He saw no prospect of peace, and thought that a good many men would be killed in Egypt. To Major-General Ross he writes in the same letter:—'We shall prepare for the land defence of England by much wild and capricious expenditure of money, and if the enemy should ever elude the vigilance of our wooden walls, we shall, after all, make a bad figure.'

A few days subsequently he was called on to proceed to France, in order to negotiate the Peace of Amiens; and with a hope that he might still give an old friend 'as good partridge shooting as Suffolk can afford' at no distant date, he set out on his diplomatic mission

CHAPTER IX

THE PEACE OF AMIENS

THE principal points in the negotiations which ended in the Peace of Amiens are matters of history. But a short account of them may be given in this chapter, inasmuch as Indian affairs were the subject of a brief discussion by Bonaparte and as they illustrate the capacity of the ex-Governor-General for dealing with politicians who were as disingenuous and subtle as any Indian prince could be. Great Britain wanted to recover some of her colonial possessions. The English negotiators at the Preliminary Treaty had been anxious that the French should evacuate Egypt. There were other serious matters for discussion regarding the Neapolitan and Roman States and the restoration of Malta to the Knights of St. John. And there was also the question of the release of prisoners in both countries and the expenses of their maintenance during captivity. Bonaparte wished for peace in order to make a better preparation for war: purposely delayed proceedings and threw the blame of the delay on England; used a haughty and dictatorial tone in his correspondence about the form and manner of the negotiations; and throughout showed his usual duplicity. As the final results are known and are available to all readers, a few incidents of the negotiations may be mentioned here, as they illustrate Cornwallis's tact in negotiation.

Cornwallis left Dover early on the morning of November 3rd, 1801, and reached Calais at ten o'clock at night, after a stormy passage of fifteen hours. He was received with all due respect and honour, and pushed on almost at once to Paris. On November the 8th he had an interview with Talleyrand, whom he distrusted as unscrupulous. According to this Prince, Bonaparte was very anxious (*empressé*) to see the English plenipotentiary. The interview took place on the 10th of the month, Talleyrand being present, and we have this description of the meeting in a letter to Lord Hawkesbury.

'Bonaparte was gracious to the highest degree. He enquired particularly after His Majesty and the state of his health, and spoke of the British nation in terms of great respect, intimating that as long as we remained friends, there would be no interruption of the peace of Europe. I told him that the horrors which succeeded the Revolution had created a general alarm; that all the neighbouring nations dreaded the contagion; that when, for the happiness of mankind, and of France in particular, he was called to fill his present situation, we knew him only as a hero and a conqueror: but the good order and tranquillity which the country now enjoyed made us respect him as a statesman and a legislator, and had removed our apprehensions of having connection and intercourse with France.' There were fireworks and illuminations in the evening. The crowd of spectators was orderly. Nothing but expressions of civility were heard as Cornwallis drove through the streets, and when he went to the opera a few nights afterwards he was 'greeted with loud and general acclamations.'

Lord Cornwallis, from his early travels on the Continent, must have acquired a very fair command of the French language, and at one time he evidently expected to have several additional interviews with the First Consul. But for some reason this plan was not fully carried out, and the English Plenipotentiary was referred for the whole discussion to Joseph Bonaparte, who had the character of a 'well-meaning although not a very able man.' The two diplomatists began their conference at Paris but soon shifted their ground to Amiens. Before leaving the French capital Cornwallis had one more conference with Bonaparte without the presence of a third person. It lasted half-an-hour. Bonaparte's views and wishes are given by Cornwallis in another letter to Lord Hawkesbury as follows:—

'He began the conversation by assurances of his earnest desire for peace, and avowed that it was much wanted for his country, which had entirely lost its commerce, and in a great degree exhausted its pecuniary resources, adding, "You see that I conceal nothing, *et que je parle franchement*": he desired only to adhere, in the arrangement of the Definitive Treaty, to the full intent and meaning of the preliminary articles, and as I should find M. Joseph Bonaparte a just and fair man, he made no doubt that everything would be speedily adjusted.'

The remainder of this memorable interview was occupied with the principal matters in dispute: the departure of the French fleet for St. Domingo, and the chagrin of the First Consul at our remonstrances on this expedition: the indemnity to the Stadtholder and the House of Orange: a suggested provision for the King of Sardinia: the strange proposal to admit a Russian garrison into Malta, which Bonaparte justly characterised as equally mischievous and detrimental to England and France: the cession of the island of Tobago: the charge for the maintenance of prisoners: and the desire of the First Consul to negotiate with a Nawáb for the cession of a 'few leagues of territory round Pondicherry.' To this latter proposal Cornwallis at once replied by stating that there was no Nawáb with whom the French could treat, and that any such addition of territory would only tend to embroil the two nations. *Vous êtes bien dur*, was Bonaparte's reply. He added that if there could be a mutual agreement for the removal of disaffected or dangerous persons from either country, he would be quite willing to send United Irishmen away.

So ended this conference. The discussion was renewed at Amiens by Joseph Bonaparte and Cornwallis. It continued all through December, 1801, and January and February, 1802. The serious part of the correspondence is here relieved by a lively letter from Lord Brome to his father's friend, General Hope. He, Lord Brome, had been occupied with Parisian sights in the morning and with dinners of forty and fifty people in the evening, who had 'the dress of mountebanks and the manners of assassins.' He had seen an odd mixture of ladies, amongst whom was Talleyrand's mistress, whom he calls Mme. Grand, and who was, of course, the divorced wife of M. Le Grand, who figured in a celebrated case in the Supreme Court of Calcutta in connection with Philip Francis. Every Anglo-Indian knows the exclamation of a Puisne Judge of that tribunal to his colleague, Sir Elijah Impey, C.J., when the latter cast Francis in damages to the extent of 50,000 rupees: 'Siccas, brother Impey! siccas!'

The sessions of the Corps Législatif did not fill Lord Brome with reverence:—'No puppet-show could be more ridiculous.' 'There came in a man dressed in a sort of mountebank dress, who, it was natural to imagine, was going to exhibit on the tight rope, but who turned out to be Citizen Chaptal, Minister of the Interior.' This man, the son of a small apothecary, became distinguished as a chemist, and was amongst the first persons who set up large factories for the manufacture of sugar from beet-root. And then the negotiations went slowly on. Joseph Bonaparte, in the opinion of Cornwallis, improved into a 'very sensible, modest, gentlemanlike man, totally free from diplomatic chicanery, and fair and open in all his dealings.' To a request from Lady Spencer that certain articles of glass might pass free of duty, Cornwallis found time to answer that though averse to all contraband traffic, he would take care that her glass should be brought over with his own baggage, on his return. Of the society at Amiens an amusing picture is given in a letter from Colonel Nightingale, who was one of the suite of the British Plenipotentiary, to Ross. The majority of the male sex at Amiens might, without deviating from truth, be called rogues, and many of the females, with equal propriety, something worse.

Joseph Bonaparte was the best among them, although he had not the manners of a gentleman. His wife was a vulgar little woman, without anything to say for herself. She had been Mdlle. Clary, and lived down to 1845. To the Prefect was applied the epithet given by one of the friends of Charles Surface to the picture of Sir Oliver. This man had been a member of the National Convention and had voted for the death of the king. Cornwallis, as might be expected, was very civil to all these local notabilities: gave large dinners twice a week, as he had done at

Calcutta; and rode out every day when not prevented by the weather or by swellings in the legs, of which there had already been an ominous mention in some of the letters from Dublin.

Throughout January, February, and the greater part of March, 1802, the terms of the proposed Treaty were sifted, analysed, and pulled to pieces till the patience of Cornwallis was nearly exhausted. 'What can be expected,' he writes, 'from a nation naturally overbearing and insolent, when all the powers of Europe are prostrating themselves at its feet and supplicating for forgiveness and future favour, except one little island, which by land at least is reduced to a strict, and at best, a very inconvenient defensive?' More than once he was in dread of the renewal of a bloody war or the alternative of the dishonour and degradation of his country. He wished 'himself again in the backwoods of America, at two hundred miles distance from his supplies, or on the banks of the Cauvery without the means of either using or withdrawing his heavy artillery.' At length, however, every difficulty was surmounted in one way or other: the stipulations in favour of the Prince of Orange, the articles relating to the Porte, the arrangement about Malta and Portugal, with some compromises and concessions, were all definitely settled. The Peace was concluded and the Declaration signed on March 25th, 1802. The signatures were affixed to the Treaty a few days afterwards. Almost anticipating an expression employed by another British statesman more than seventy years afterwards, Cornwallis had hoped for a 'peace that will not dishonour the country,' and one 'that would afford as reasonable a prospect of a future safety as the present very extraordinary circumstances of Europe would admit.'

The table on which this Treaty was signed is, writes the editor of the Cornwallis *Correspondence*, still preserved in the Hôtel de Ville at Amiens. At one end of the apartment there is a full-length picture of the Plenipotentiaries and their suites. The portrait of Cornwallis is not unlike but the painting is indifferent. 'In the background an English officer is cordially embracing one of the French suite.

CHAPTER X

RETURN TO INDIA. POLICY. DEATH

ON his return from Amiens Cornwallis found something to interest him in the elections, and his letters are amusingly illustrative of the way in which such political events were managed in those times. There was an election for the county of Suffolk, in which there 'was reason to expect the most perfect unanimity.' This election had to give way to the claims of the races at Newmarket, and was postponed for three days in consequence. But there was rather more excitement about the return of two members for the borough of Eye. Cornwallis is careful to state that his party neither bribed nor treated in what was practically a pocket borough, and that a majority had been secured of four to one incontestable voters, after deducting paupers and those who had purchased meal at a reduced price during the scarcity. The elections ended satisfactorily by the return of two members of the Cornwallis family who each polled 114 votes, their opponents obtaining fifteen apiece.

In November, 1802, Cornwallis writes: 'I am still

equal to a pretty good day's fag in shooting, but I think that I rather train off as a marksman; this sport, however, amuses me, and is an inducement to take exercise, which I am persuaded is right.' The affairs of India again occupied his attention. He was consulted about a suggestion for giving Jonathan Duncan, who had been a successful administrator of the Province of Benares, and who was then Governor of Bombay, a seat in Council in Bengal, and placing him at the head of the whole Revenue department. At the same time, too, he seems to have been asked privately whether he would care again to go to Ireland as Commander-in-Chief. Nothing came of this, nor is there any trace of the offer in the State Papers.

He sat to Hoppner the well-known portrait painter, and in this fashion some months passed away. But he was quite ready to do the State further service, and even Culford, with its rural pleasures and occupations, began to pall. 'To sit down quietly by myself, without occupation or object, to contemplate the dangers of my country, with the prospect of being a mere cypher, without arms in my hands,' was not pleasing to a man whose previous life had been usefully and actively spent. In a letter written in September, 1803, he notes that it was not his fault that he did not again go to Ireland. He would not have meddled with politics, and would have been entirely under the Lord-Lieutenant. As it was he considered himself to be 'laid quietly on the shelf.' As Constable of the

Tower he was plagued with applications some of which must have been rather absurd, and the King himself was anxious for his return to Ireland.

About the end of 1804, Cornwallis expressed some anxiety as to the success of Lord Wellesley's policy in India, an anxiety which was not justified by the result. And probably owing to these views and to wishes expressed either by the Ministry or the Court of Directors, or both, he began seriously to consider about his return to that country. The Court of Directors for some time past had been alarmed at Lord Wellesley's vigorous foreign policy. Castlereagh at the Board of Control had taken fright, and even Pitt was carried away and committed himself to a hasty opinion that the Governor-General had acted imprudently and illegally. So, after a little more consideration, Cornwallis decided again to accept the offer of the Governor-Generalship. He was to discuss Indian politics with the President of the Board of Control in the winter, and to arrange for a landing in Bengal by the latter end of the south-west Monsoon.

He was then entering on his sixty-seventh year. To men of the present generation, accustomed to weigh all the chances of health and efficiency in an Indian climate with regard to their individual constitutions, it seems extraordinary that no medical opinion should have been taken. Swellings in the feet and increasing weakness of body had been apparent for some little time. He himself spoke of the adventure 'as a desperate act.' No English statesman has ever taken office in India at so advanced an age. Lord Hardinge went out as Governor-General when he was fifty-nine. Lord Lawrence, after a long previous service as a Bengal Civilian, had had six years' comparative rest in England, and became Viceroy at fifty-four. Other statesmen, such as Wellesley and Dalhousie, were in their thirty-fifth or thirty-sixth year. But duty was paramount with Cornwallis. He had not sought the high office, but he would not refuse to accede to the combined request of a political associate and his old masters the Court of Directors.

Dr. Dick, his medical attendant in India on the previous occasion, offered his services in the same capacity. But Cornwallis thought the embarkation of 'himself on the Medusa Frigate, attended by his physician,' would sound ridiculous. In the present day every Viceroy has long had a physician as an officer of his suite, just as he has a Private Secretary, a Military Secretary, and four or more Aides-de-Camp. Directly his intended departure became known he was overwhelmed with 'absurd and ridiculous applications.' If the Company 'was to hire forty large vessels' they could not carry one half the persons who had asked for situations in which they might eat a piece of bread. Cornwallis left England in the spring of 1805, and after touching at Madras, landed in Calcutta on the 29th of July of that year.

Events had succeeded each other with startling rapidity since he left the country in the autumn of 1793. That the mild and pacific policy of his immediate successor, carried on with the avowed object of maintaining peace by the mere balance of power between the various native states, had failed in its aims and was unsuited to the age and country, is now almost universally admitted. With the arrival of the Wellesleys the whole scene was transformed. In six years' time the British armies, directed by one brother in the Council and commanded by another in the field, were everywhere triumphant. The capital of Tipú Sultán was stormed. The French battalions at Haidarábád were disbanded, and the Nizám, from an envious rival or a halting friend, became an obedient ally. The Maráthá powers that had risen on the ruins of the crumbling Mughal Empire, were shattered. The Madras Presidency had swelled to its present dimensions. We had acquired what are now known as the North-Western Provinces of India. We had the Peshwá for our vassal. Monson's disastrous retreat before Holkar, and Lake's failure to take Bhartpur, for years afterwards the never-failing subjects of jeers and gibes in the bázárs of India and amongst the disaffected classes, had been the only undertakings not crowned with a splendid success. It was not likely that masterly combinations could be carried out without straining the financial and military resources of British India. And when Sindhia, in spite of his overthrow, was anxious to renew warlike operations, and Holkar had never been subdued, Cornwallis appeared on the scene with orders from home to substitute negotiations and diplomacy for war, and almost to abandon the proud position of the Paramount Power which, foreshadowed by Hastings for the Company, in spite of doubts and hesitations, had been attained by Wellesley.

The first act of Cornwallis on his arrival was to make preparations for a visit to the Upper Provinces. He wrote to Lord Lake to warn him against engaging in any acts of aggression and renewal of military operations. He informed the Secret Committee that he trusted, on arriving in Upper India, to terminate by negotiations and without any sacrifice of honour, a contest in which the most brilliant successes could afford no solid benefit, and which threatened the gravest financial complications. To the Court of Directors he explained that he should be compelled to detain the ships carrying treasure to China, and to apply to Madras for five lacks of rupees to carry on his government. He had fully made up his mind that subsidiary treaties were a mistake, and that they burdened the Indian Government with useless native dependants and allies. He expected no advantage from a contest with Holkar and Sindhia, as they had no territory to lose. And as a proof of his strong feeling on this point, he was anxious to give up the alliances with the Ját chief of Bhartpur, the Rájá of Macheri, and the Ráná of Gohad. There was considerable correspondence in regard to the last-mentioned State, and it is only fair to the memory and character of Cornwallis to state here in his own words the exact policy which he intended to pursue and which has been more or less condemned by Anglo-Indian historians. In a letter to Lord Lake, written about a fortnight before his own death, he fully explains his meaning and intentions.

'1. To make over to Sindhia the possessions of Gwalior and Gohad.

'2. To transfer to him, according to the provisions of the treaty of peace, the districts of Dholpur, Bári, and Rajkerrie, and to account to Sindhia for the collections from these districts since the peace.

'I am aware that this is not to be considered in the light of a concession, but I am willing to relinquish that stipulation of the treaty which prohibits Sindhia from stationing a force in these districts, an object which I should suppose to be highly desirable to that chieftain.

'3. The eventual restoration of the Jainagar tribute, amounting, as I understand, to the annual sum of 3 lacks of rupees.

'4. To require from Sindhia his consent to the abrogation of the pensions, and to the resumption of the Jaghírs in the Doáb, established by the treaty of peace.

'5. To require from Sindhia the relinquishment of his claim to the arrears of his pension.

'6. To demand a compensation for the public and private losses sustained by the plunder of the Residency.

'7. To require Sindhia to make a provision for the Ráná of Gohad to the extent of 2½ or 3 lacks of rupees, which I should conceive should be amply sufficient.'

He goes on to say that he proposes to cede nothing to Sindhia which it is any object to retain: that Sindhia must understand that the British Government does not admit his right to either Gohad or Gwalior, and that the transfer of these places is an entirely gratuitous one on our part; and that he was disposed to act in concert with Sindhia, as an ally against Holkar. And he was also prepared to restore to Holkar territory conquered by the British forces.

He declared that his object was to restore to the Native States that confidence in the justice and moderation of the British Government which past events had considerably impaired, and which appeared essential to the security and tranquillity of the British dominions. And then follow about three pages regarding the claims of the Ráná of Gohad. The position of this chieftain was peculiar, and from a most trustworthy source it may be stated as follows.

The Governor of Gohad, named Ambají Inglia, had, in 1803, thrown off his allegiance to Sindhia, and joined the British forces on the understanding that he was to surrender to them the fort of Gwalior, and certain districts which the Government intended to confer on the Ráná. Thirty years before this time Warren Hastings had made a treaty with the Ráná, and the joint forces of the Ráná and the English then retook Gwalior, which Sindhia had previously seized. The Ráná subsequently was thrown over, on the ground that he had been guilty of treachery, and then Sindhia retook Gwalior and Gohad. This latter place is some twenty-eight miles from Gwalior, now Sindhia's capital, and the Ját chiefs had established themselves there in the beginning of the eighteenth century, like so many others in troublous times.

At the close of the successful campaign of 1803 the position of Sindhia and Gohad was this. Sindhia, by the Treaty of Surjee Angengam, had agreed to renounce all claim on his feudatories with whom the British Government had made treaties. The Ráná of Gohad was clearly one of those feudatories, but taking advantage of the wording of the treaty and of the Ráná's recent conduct, Sindhia contended that the treaties alluded to which he was bound to respect, could not include the Ráná, inasmuch as his pretensions had been extinguished and his territories had been in Sindhia's possession for thirty years. The obvious reply to this claim was, that recent conquest and separate treaties with the Ráná concluded in 1803 and 1804, by Lord Wellesley, had reversed their positions, and had restored the Ráná's old rights and claims to our protection[1]. But Cornwallis was so deeply impressed with the necessity for concluding a general pacification of the country, so convinced of the inability of the Ráná to manage his possessions, collect the revenues, and preserve tranquillity, and so apprehensive of the dangers and vexations of a direct British Administration forced on us by failure of the native rule, that he was quite ready to annul or disregard the stipulation in the treaty, and to restore Gohad and Gwalior to Sindhia. It is true that he intended to compensate the Ráná for this loss, and within a few months after the death of Cornwallis, his temporary successor, Sir George Barlow, granted to the Ráná the sovereignty over the districts of Dholpur, Bári, and Rajkerrie. The Chambal river became the boundary between Dholpur and Sindhia. Rájá Kirat Sing, of Dholpur, took rank as one of the Rájput Princes, lived to a great age, died in 1836, and was succeeded by a chief who protected British fugitives and behaved loyally in the mutiny of 1857.

For this one special provision and for the retransfer of Gwalior to the Maráthás, there is really a good deal, but for the general and prompt reversal of Wellesley's policy there is very little, to be said. The Ráná had no claim as the representative of an ancient family. From a mere landholder he had

[1] Sir C. Aitchison's *Treaties*, vol. iv.

become a chieftain, and the loss of Gohad was made up to him by the gain of Dholpur. The cession to Gwalior was followed by the discontinuance of the pensions paid by Government to Sindhia's officers, amounting to fifteen lacks of rupees, but was coupled with other stipulations very advantageous to the Maráthás. They will be clearly seen by the subjoined excellent summary taken from the *Treaties and Engagements* of Sir C. Aitchison:—

'A Treaty was concluded on 23rd of November, 1805, which confirmed the Treaty of Sarge Angengaum, except what might be altered by this Treaty, ceded Gwalior and Gohad to Sindhia, abolished the pensions of fifteen lacks a year paid by Government to Sindhia's officers, constituted the Chambal the northern boundary of Sindhia's territory, deprived Sindhia of all claim to tribute from Búndi or any State north of the Chambal and east of Kotah, bound the British not to make treaties with Údaipur, Jodhpur, Kotah, or other chiefs tributary to Sindhia in Málwá or Mewár, or to interfere with the arrangements which Sindhia might make in regard to them; and granted a pension of four lacks a year to Sindhia, and Jaghírs of two lacks to his wife Baiza Bái, and one lack to his daughter, Chamna Bái[1].'

Whatever admiration may be entertained for Cornwallis, his character, motives, and internal reforms, it

[1] Vol. v. p. 200.

is impossible not to condemn the foreign policy which he sketched and which his successor completed. Sindhia had no special claim on our forbearance and gratitude. He had invited defeat by our forces, and had intrigued with our secret and open foes. The abandonment of the high-spirited Rájput Princes to Maráthá rapacity was denounced by Lord Lake, and was not creditable to the British name. Concessions to Holkar who had deserved nothing at our hands, only served to whet his appetite for plunder and to stimulate his insolent and revengeful spirit. The policy of 1805 had the effect of 'allowing the whole of Hindustán, beyond its own boundaries, to become a scene of fearful strife, lawless plunder, and frightful desolation for many succeeding years, until the same horrors invaded its own sacred precincts, and involved it in expensive and perilous warfare, the result of which was its being obliged to assume what it had so long mischievously declined, the avowed supremacy over all the States and Princes of Hindustán.'

This policy has been condemned by historians and commentators, as well as by statesmen, soldiers, and diplomatists; by Mill and his editor, H. H. Wilson, and by Thornton; by Lord Lake and Sir John Malcolm. The mischief was done and the loss of influence was not regained for a decade. It was not till the conclusion of an expensive and protracted campaign, that the Indian Government was replaced in the position where it had been left by Wellesley. The blame of this weak and unfortunate policy must be divided between Cornwallis and Barlow, between the Court of Directors and the Board of Control.

The end was now nigh. The Governor-General had assumed his office on July 30th. The Marquess of Wellesley did not leave India till the 29th of August, so that there must have been some time for the two statesmen to interchange views and to discuss all present and future policy. On the 8th of August Cornwallis was at Barrackpur, and for nearly two months his state barge was being towed slowly against the current of the Ganges, swollen by the rains, in his progress to the Upper Provinces. During this time he was constantly writing or dictating State Papers, and whatever condemnation may be passed on their substance, it is not possible to discern in the style any traces of a failing intellect. Read from his point of view the diction and reasoning are still clear and precise. It was hoped that the air of the river, which has occasionally saved the lives of Indian officers struck down by fever or dysentery, would have restored him to something like health and activity. But it was too late. His last public letter is dated Sept. 23rd. After that we are dependent on the letters of secretaries and friends. There was a slight rally on the 25th. On the 5th of October he expired at Ghâzípur. He had been removed on the 29th of September from his boat to a house at that station.

The inhabitants of Calcutta and other residents in

different parts of India were profoundly moved. At a meeting convened by the sheriff of Calcutta, held on October 29th, it was resolved that in order to express the public sense of his virtues, a memorial should be erected in his honour. The native inhabitants sent a letter to the Chairman of the same meeting signifying their grateful sense of his just and honourable administration, and intimating that they regarded him as their guardian and benefactor. Copies of the resolutions passed at this meeting were sent to Madras and Bombay, to Ceylon, Penang, and Fort Marlborough. Subscriptions were invited and a committee was formed. A funeral sermon was preached at Madras by the order of the Governor, Lord William Bentinck, on the 9th of November. The text was taken from the 24th verse of the 35th chapter of the Second Book of Chronicles, 'And all Judah and Jerusalem mourned for Josiah.' A correspondent of the *Calcutta Gazette* prefaced some verses to his memory by the well-known and well-timed quotation from the *Agricola* of Tacitus, 'Finis vitae ejus nobis luctuosus, amicis tristis, extraneis etiam ignotisque non sine curâ fuit.' On the 17th of November, what was termed 'an eloquent and appropriate sermon' was preached by the Rev. N. Wade, at Bombay, preceded by a choral service which 'for taste, judgment, and execution, far exceeded anything of the kind in India.' The text chosen, not perhaps very happily, was from the 21st verse of the 9th chapter of the First Book of the Maccabees, 'How is the valiant man fallen, that delivered Israel.'

Cornwallis lies at Gházípur, in a monument described as a domed quasi-Grecian building, with a marble statue by Flaxman[1]. There is another statue in the Town Hall of Calcutta, and an excellent full-length portrait hangs on the walls of the Council Chamber at Government House in the same city. He is painted in uniform, and has for his companions Clive; Warren Hastings, in knee-breeches and velvet coat; Lord Wellesley; Lord Minto, with a scroll in his hand; and, last of all, Mr. Adam, who, in the interval between the departure of the Marquess of Hastings and the arrival of Lord Amherst, caused J. S. Buckingham to be deported for an offence against the censorship of the press. The statue of Cornwallis in the Town Hall is by Bacon, junior. It is not one of the sculptor's happiest efforts; and the garb of an ancient Roman, though in the taste of the day, does not set off the Governor-General to advantage. The two female figures at the base of the statue, with a mirror and a serpent, signifying justice and truth, belong to no particular age or country. From a cornucopia are poured out all sorts of Indian vegetables and fruits—the pine-apple and the custard-apple, mangoes and *líchís,* Indian corn and rice-stalks; and we discern a lion's skin, a club, and a bundle of arrows. The work is inferior to the bronze statue of

[1] *Imperial Gazetteer of India,* vol. v. p. 70.

Lord William Bentinck, in the open air in front of the same Town Hall, and far below Foley's splendid equestrian statue of Lord Hardinge.

The character of Cornwallis has been drawn by more than one historian, and not always with fairness. In Thornton's *History of British India*, his mental constitution is described as the highest order of commonplace. He is said to have been entirely destitute of originality, and to have represented the spirit, the opinions, and the prejudices of his own age. This historian adds that, although he enjoyed an extraordinary degree of reputation during his lifetime, its artificial brilliancy soon passed away.

Mill, while admitting the generous policy of the Permanent Settlement, declares that it was dictated in some measure by prejudice, and attributes to Cornwallis, himself an aristocrat, the intention of establishing an aristocracy on the European model. No one who has carefully studied the public and private lives of the eminent men who have been selected from the two great political parties of England and have ruled India at eventful times, would place Cornwallis on the same platform as Wellesley and Dalhousie, or would compare him for ability, vigour, and energy to that servant of the East India Company who, from a writer, became Governor-General, and was not rewarded by a diadem. But there was nothing commonplace about Cornwallis; and if in some points he reflected and acted on the opinions of his time, in others he was far ahead of it. In his contempt for jobbery; his determination to place the Company's servants, whom he transformed from merchants to administrators, above the reach of temptation; in his anxiety to protect native rights and interests; in constructive ability and in tenacity of purpose, he may challenge a comparison with some of the most eminent men who have ruled India.

His aristocratical prejudices—if they be so considered—were really just what suited his position and aims. It may be truly said that they cannot be cast aside by any statesman who thoroughly comprehends the peoples whom he has to govern, and the problems which he ought to solve. There is nothing democratic in the various strata of Indian society. From its earliest traditions to its recent history it has been the sanctuary of privilege. Its tribes worship pomp and pageantry, and are reconciled to an apparent inequality, over which every man of talent and capacity hopes to triumph. It may be taken as an axiom that the general sense of the natives is in favour of marked gradations of rank, and of exemption from restraints and restrictions, while at the same time a value is set on impartial justice, inviolate good faith, and incorruptible integrity. Guilds and fraternities, associations of traders, community of interests between co-parcenary communities, are not democratic, but if anything oligarchical; and caste, in all its endless ramifications, is a symbol of honour and not a badge of disgrace.

Cornwallis may perhaps be best described as a statesman on whom the Ministry of the day could always rely. His patriotism, his regard for discipline, his sense of duty to the State, were the qualities which attained their fullest development in Wellington. A statesman who purified and reconstituted the civil administration of a great Empire; who promulgated a code of law on lines which were followed by more experienced legislators; who carried out the Union of Ireland in despite of avowed enemies and of injudicious friends; who induced a military despot to agree to a treaty, in which every step might have led to a snare or a pitfall; possessed qualities which ought to mitigate censure, and did much that in balancing accounts should be placed to his credit.

Cornwallis overflows in Minutes and State Papers, as well as in private correspondence. His writings are not, like those of Wellesley and Dalhousie, close in reasoning, splendid from their sustained eloquence, and broad and far-reaching in aim; but they are replete with sound sense and right feeling, and his deliverances on thorny and intricate questions prove that he had the faculty of apprehending the salient points of new subjects, for which he could not have been prepared by his previous learning in Parliament or in camp. Moreover, his life was one of almost uninterrupted devotion to duty and work. Other statesmen, who before and after him filled a similar office in India, have returned home, and have taken comparatively but a slight share in politics. Some succumbed to the rapid death which carried off Achilles, or were victims to the slow decay which undermined the strength and vigour of Tithonus. But Cornwallis had little or no rest. From America to the Continent; from England to India; from India to Ireland and back to India to die, his whole career was one of duty and self-sacrifice. It may be added that his private life was estimable and pure. His letters to relations and friends breathe a spirit of the truest friendship and regard, and it is a trite quotation, 'Bonum virum facile crederes: magnum libenter.'

The family of Cornwallis is extinct in the male line. The son of the Governor-General—the Viscount Brome, mentioned in the correspondence—succeeded his father, as second Marquess, and died leaving no male issue, in 1823. His sister, the Lady Mary Cornwallis, married, in 1815, Mark Singleton, then an ensign in the guards. At the death of the second Marquess, the earldom passed to the Bishop of Lichfield, and then to his son James. At his death, in 1852, the title became extinct. But the descendants of Cornwallis are still to be found in the following families. The eldest daughter of the second Marquess married the third Lord Braybrooke. Two of the sons of this marriage fell in the Crimea—one at Balaclava, and the other at Inkerman. The present peer, the fifth Lord Braybrooke, is great-grandson to the Governor-General. Another descendant, Charles Cornwallis

Ross, who also died in the Crimea, was the grandson of the second Marquess, by Lady Mary Ross. Lady Jemima, another daughter of the same peer, married the third Earl of St. Germans. One son of this marriage, Captain Eliot, was killed at Inkerman. The present Earl St. Germans and the Hon. Charles Eliot, issue of the same marriage, are still alive. Those who have not yet ceased to believe in the hereditary character of worth, may be glad to know that the line of the Founder of all sound Indian Administration has not quite passed away

INDEX

APPENDIX

[*Note on the object of this memoir and the authorities referred to by the Author.*]

THE Irish administration of Cornwallis has been designedly excluded from this memoir, the object being to show what Cornwallis effected as a Ruler of India. And in this view chapters have been added descriptive of the extension of the Perpetual Settlement to other Provinces besides Bengal and Behar, and of the supplementary legislation which was found indispensable to the completion of the same Settlement in the Lower Provinces. The sources of information to which the Author has had recourse are the following:—

The Cornwallis Correspondence. Edited, with accurate and copious notes, by Charles Ross, Esq., 3 vols., 1858.

The celebrated *Fifth Report of the House of Commons on the Affairs of India*, 1812.

The Regulations and Acts of the Government of India from 1793 to 1859 inclusive.

The Judicial Decisions of the Sadr Diwání Adálat from 1793 to 1862 *and the subsequent Decisions of the High Court of Calcutta.*

3 vols. of manuscript notes taken between 1857 and 1860 inclusive, by the Author of this memoir, during a systematic and unofficial enquiry into the rents, rights, and privileges of the Tenant-proprietors of Bengal and into village and agricultural customs.

Calcutta Review, 1857 to 1859; articles by the Author on *Life in the Rice Fields*, *Bengal Village Biographies*, and the *Owner of the Soil*.

Report of the Indigo Commission, 1860.

Life of Sir John Shore, First Lord Teignmouth, by his Son, 2 vols. 1843.

Lives of Indian Officers, by the late Sir John Kaye, K.C.S.I.

Lives of Eminent British Commanders, in Vol. II of Dr. Lardner's Cabinet Cyclopædia.

Selections from *Calcutta Gazettes*, by the Author, 3 vols.

Revenue Handbook, by the late James H. Young, Bengal C. S.

The Imperial Gazetteer, by Sir William W. Hunter, K.C.S.I., C.I.E.

The N.-W. Provinces Gazetteer.

Reports of the Officers of the Survey in Bengal and Behar; especially those of Capt. W. Sherwill.

Report of the Government of Bengal on the Proposed Amendment of the Law of Landlord and Tenant, 1883.

Two volumes (anonymous) on the *Zamíndárí Settlement*, 1879.

Divers other Blue Books and *Reports*.

THE END.